This book is my learning years, my travels on a very low budget and finding the right bike. They are good times, busy times, happy times and fun times. To travel is to learn. To travel is to appreciate. Travel is to reason. Never think that to travel must be around the world, travel is around the next corner, the next bend in the road, the next hill you climb. The people you meet are a journey in life. To share is to love. To love is to share. I am so fortunate, my bikes have taught me so much and given pleasure to others I met. My home is always with me. (My bike), I hope you can share my travels and experiences with me.

Mark Cheney.

Thank you Susan for all the help you have given me in writing this book

STILL LOOKING FOR
THE HORIZON
A TRAVELLER'S STORY

MARK CHENEY

The Early Years
My Dreaming Years
My Learning Years
Mark Cheney

Published 2014 by arima publishing

www.arimapublishing.com

ISBN 978 1 84549 622 7
© Mark Cheney 2014

All rights reserved

This book is copyright. Subject to statutory exception and to provisions of relevant collective licensing agreements, no part of this publication may be reproduced, stored in a retrieval system, or transmitted in any form or by any means, without the prior written permission of the author.

Printed and bound in the United Kingdom

Typeset in Garamond

This book is sold subject to the conditions that it shall not, by way of trade or otherwise, be lent, re-sold, hired out, or otherwise circulated without the publisher's prior consent in any form of binding or cover other than that which it is published and without a similar condition including this condition being imposed on the subsequent purchaser.

In this work of fiction, the characters, places and events are either the product of the author's imagination or they are used entirely fictitiously. The moral rights of the author have been asserted. Any resemblance to actual persons, living or dead, is purely coincidental.

Swirl is an imprint of arima publishing.

arima publishing
ASK House, Northgate Avenue
Bury St Edmunds, Suffolk IP32 6BB
t: (+44) 01284 700321

www.arimapublishing.com

EFFORTLESS TRAVEL

My boyhood dreams were effortless travel. It can only be a bike. Working to keep my family, making my business work but always there during my little free time that (itch) the plan, the hope, that one day, maybe I would cross the channel to France maybe even further. My real dreams as a lad were of this long road I would glide along effortlessly. They were wonderful dreams.

The reason you latch onto some things as a child is because you see it around, hear it, talk of it. I know the reason why I don't like some things. My Father was an aircraft engineer during World War 2. He worked on the Gloucester Gladiator, the Hawker Typhoon and my interest in planes and war machines came from him.

As a little boy November the 5th Bonfire Night came and went. The next morning, um interesting, ooh, look a firework! It promptly exploded in my hand taking off two of my nails. You know I don't like fireworks or for that matter petrol blowlamps. Watching my Father starting his to me was a delight. Well it looks easy no problem. One day armed with my stolen matches I decided to light his lamp. I know you have to pump it so I did. The flames were 3 feet high and I am sat on my haunches looking at it. I ran away from home but was found two hours later hiding behind a wall at the Vicarage. Why the Vicarage I have no idea maybe I though the Vicar would save me from the wroth of my Father. As one grows older one learns about life. I think I would have been safer at home. I was returned home and no one said a word about the blowlamp. My Dad's shed was still intact. How does that work? I don't like petrol blowlamps!

As long as I can remember an old motorbike stood under a sheet in the garden. Slowly it was transformed from a rusty wreck to a shiny bike with an engine that runs. I like bikes.

DELIVERING MY NEWSPAPERS

Effortless travel was looming in front of me, a motor- bike. Having had the experience of bikes from an early age, I was delivering my newspapers one evening. I dropped the paper as normal and turning to walk back to the gate I noticed a door open to a shed. There was the front of a motorbike, I had a look in and there it was in all its glory. I walked back to the front door and knocked. I only ever saw the lady on Fridays when I called for the money. She said "Hello it's not Friday". "No" I said, "I just noticed your bike in the shed do you want to sell it"? She replied "well it's my Husbands I can ask him for you". I though this was great and skipped out of the gate. The next evening as I dropped off her paper she came to the door. My husband said that you could buy his bike for the price of five pounds. Oh I said, "great it will take me a few weeks to save all that, I will have it and thank you very much". Within a few weeks I was stood at the door with my five pounds. Having taken with me my friend. Do you think you can manage it? "Oh no problem" we said, fortunately for us the trip home was all down hill. So we could free wheel home. Once out of the gate and the lady was out of view we climbed on. We ride pushbikes so we thought there would not be much difference. We were about to learn a lesson. Down a narrow lane we went onto the hill through the village. We seemed to gather speed quite quickly. Then came the tricky bit, left into our lane, with both brakes full on we were slowing up, but not slowing up quite enough to turn into the lane. I am shouting to my friend drag your feet. Too late we hit the bank, the bike went on and we were thrown off, watching it start off down the field. Fortunately it hit a big molehill and crashed to the ground, PEW that was close. We were fine not a scratch. We picked the bike up and walked with it and finally came out farther down the lane. Not giving up we climbed on and away we went again arriving in one piece and very happy about it. When my Dad came home from work he came straight down to us, um it's a Sunbeam a good make. I can get that going OK, so that evening it burst into life, my Dad was smart.

After a few days of looking at her I started to strip off everything I though we wouldn't need, mudguards, lights, toolboxes, stand. I stripped it to nothing. This would make it lighter to enable my friend and I to push it the half-mile to a field, ride it around until it ran out of petrol and then we would push it back.

But one day being smart my pal and I were pushing it on the road up a hill. I new it would not start so I popped it into gear and dropped the clutch, the last thing we expected it to do was start, (it did) and it was away dragging the pair of us up the road. As it leapt away the throttle opened until we couldn't keep up. Letting the bike go it crashed to the ground taking us with it. This resulted in our hands and knees cut and bleeding, and tears.

Mopping ourselves with my shirt we sat in the road. After the bleeding eased up we carried on pushing the bike to our field where all was forgotten until, we ran out of petrol and pushed the bike home. It took my Mother half an hour to pick the gravel out of my knees, accompany by my howling. (Mothers!)

MY TRANSPORT TO WORK

For a year I rode my cycle to work. I was 15 years old and not wanting to wait a whole year before acquiring my motorcycle license but I did. In-between I rode my old bike around the field most weekends. My 16th birthday arrived and I went with my Dad to purchase a 1939 350cc AJS. THIS WAS FREEDOM. After a year on my faithful AJS I took my first session, on headlights that come around the corner without dipping them. I had just left the local town after going to the cinema with my first girl friend who I only ever met at the Cinema or in the local park where we amused ourselves for a couple of hours and then went home. We had no idea what we were doing, just something was telling us that would be the way to go.

With headlights dazzling, you can't see were you are going so consequently you don't stop until you hit something. In my case it was the curb, the bike went one way and I went the other. I lay in the road looking up at the stars. The car had long gone so by the very dim lights of my bike I got up and found it. Well it seemed OK. I picked it up and yes it was OK. I gave it a kick and away it went, but heavens it sounds a bit loud and to my amazement I had lost both silencers. I walked back down the road a little bit and found them. They had cooled between me crashing and the time I found them so I stuffed them down my coat started her up and away off home, ooh it sounds good. I parked up at home and strolled in. I said nothing of my adventure but as I turned away from my Mum she said "good heavens what have you done to your coat"? "Well nothing, why"? "It's ripped from top to bottom". So it came out, I owned up. On inspecting the bike the next day it was found that the bike was badly bent, so it wasn't really rideable.

MY TRIALS RIDING DAYS

This meant going back to my pushbike to get me to work. This didn't last long. I had decided that I was going to be a trials rider. For those who don't understand trials riding it goes as follows:

You ride marked out sections over rough off road conditions, without putting your feet down to help you along. So after a few weeks with the financial help of my Mum and Dad, I had this very nice Cotton with a 197cc Villiers engine. I thought I was "the bee's knees"!

On weekends I would go out practising, um this seems fairly easy, so one Saturday, I took myself off to this steep bank with woodland, knowing that the local Motor Cycle Club rode there. The day was warm. I played about on this bank having great fun, down the bank and back up using the sheep tracks. After several goes I was growing in confidence, up I went into the right hand track but no, it went left at the same time turning me straight down the bank. I changed down, the back wheel locked and I hit another sheep track. The bike then took off and leapt straight into the middle of a massive blackberry bush. I was upright sat on my bike totally surrounded by the bush with no way out. Even trying to move my arms was difficult because I was completely entangled by the bush and thorns. Finally after quite a struggle I found my penknife. For an hour, I laboured with my penknife slowly cutting a path through the bush to freedom, at the same time feeding myself with a large amount of juicy blackberries (no shortage of food here). Finally, I had cut a path out through the bush. So easing myself back on the bike I gave her a kick and she started. At last I was out, no worst for ware, just a bit hot and covered in blackberry juice. Having released myself from the bush I still had to get myself up the bank and away home, again using the same route as before. I was away, bugger the not footing, I arrived at the dreaded spot and I footed my way around the bend and with a shout I broke free. Great I was away feeling rather pleased that I always carried my penknife with me. When I arrived home not a word was said, I was fine. It wasn't until the next morning as I lay in bed reading my beginners book for trials riding that I found some urgency to dash to the toilet, where I spent most of the morning. Later that day my mum said, "I don't know what you must have eaten yesterday as we haven't got a problem". I conveniently forgot to tell her about the large amount of blackberries I had consumed while extricating myself from the blackberry bush.

SOME YEARS LATER
MY FIRST LONG DISTANCE TOURER
With a self-starter.

I gradually gathered a little cash, some made from selling old bikes after a few repairs to them (hedge iron) as I refer to them these days. I would make a few pounds. Scouring the Motorcycle News each week, I would finally spot a bike that I thought would be suitable (having seen an acquaintance with that model who sang it's praises). I did not have a clue really. On one occasion I rang a chap up who was in Southampton (sorry mate it's sold). I replied O.K. He then told me that I was the third person that had said he would have it and the others had not turned up for it. "I tell you what if this chap lets me down I will give you a ring" "OK that suits me" I replied.

Well about a week later the phone rang, yes it was the Southampton man. The bloke didn't turn up. Would you still like it? I said "yes but I can't afford your price". "OK" he said, "make me an offer". I did and it was all that I could afford, one hundred pounds under the asking price. He said "OK".

Ooh shit what will the Wife say? I am doing this. Well she didn't say a lot (maybe I didn't tell my wife the price). The following weekend with the pig trailer hitched up to the car, the family were off for their day out to Southampton, stopping for a picnic on the way.

During the afternoon we found the house. The chap seemed quite amiable, and the bike quite nice, with a self-starter. The front had been damaged but repairs had been carried out, the front fairing had not been replaced. We did the deal, he seemed glad to be rid of it and that made me rather nervous. Is the engine OK? Is it bent? Well it looks OK. We loaded the bike, and went on our way. Ooh what a wonderful day out (I am sure the children loved it) well that's what I told them.

I HAVE MY FREEDOM, BMW R90S WITH A SELF STARTER, NO MORE KICKING THEM. JUST SWITCH ON AND PUSH THE BUTTON.

The bike sat in my bike room. This was the looking and thinking time. I need a screen on the front fairing, plus a rear carrier. I looked at fairings, too much money. So I took myself off to the local bike breakers and found a nearly new screen for two pounds. The carrier was one pound. "I will take them", I said.

Well if you have ever fitted a screen or carrier to a bike, when it is not supposed to fit that particular bike, then you will understand what a fiddle it was, make a bracket for this, lengthen this and finally it was on. Well it's not looking too bad. I sat on. Um OK the carrier planned would take a small tent, and my sleeping bag.

I start it up again, just switch on and push the button and away it goes. Wonderful. Oh it's talking to me.

After a few months I did several test runs (just up the road) the screen wrapped back over my hands when I reached about 90 mph. Well I think I need a few adjustments. OK back to the drawing board, more brackets and more tests. The screen is OK. The carrier no problem, it works. About three years after I had purchased miss freedom one (my R90S), I saw an Avon fairing advertised locally. I went to see it, there was a lot to it and when it was all bolted together it took a bit of lifting but I bought it. After doing some repairs, it was sprayed to match the colour of the petrol tank, silver and smoke, before it was fitted on the bike. I had to put stronger fork springs on her to take the additional weight. After I had completed fitting it, I was delighted. I could tuck in behind the lovely screen and fairing totally out of the wind, it was great. My test runs with it were good. My Beemer was fast becoming my long distance tourer. With its shiny new fairing, I was "the bee's knees".

Well I think it's ready, doing test runs, just short trips 50-60 miles. How do I break this to my Wife? There I am doing it again. Am I owned? "Would you come out for a ride"? She answered "no". "How about a weekend trip"? "No" came the reply. "I would think it would be nice to go to France on the bike", again she declined, not much help there.

GOOD MATES

Thinking I could get a cheap crossing over to France though the Motorcycle News, I asked a couple of pals if they would join me but they did not want to go, so it was with some trepidation that I booked a ferry. My travelling arrangements was set, I became a lone rider.

I had learnt after a hard lesson as a boy that travelling and being alone is not that bad, a true mate is very hard to find.

MY LEARNING YEARS

When I was a boy of about 7 years old, I had been confronted, as had many of the local boys by the village bully. His name was William Brooks about our age but twice as big. The smaller kids had taken so may hits from him that one day we all got together in a powwow, not a meeting as we were at that time into Indians in a big way. It was decided that in numbers we could get him. Several ideas were put forward. As we were Indians at that time, we could attack him with bows and arrows, someone sensibly suggested that we could hit him in the eye and that wouldn't be good. Another said he might die. Well no one seemed bothered about that at the time. One said he could get his Brothers pellet gun, but that was ruled out as we were Indians, and they had bows and arrows. After several powwows it was decided that it would have to be bare-knuckle stuff. On the fateful day we gathered 5 of us all 7 year olds. We knew that after going to his Granny's from School, at 5pm he made his way home. He would come across the fields, there was a hump in the field and we had worked out that as he came over the grassy bank we could surprise him and only have 30 yard to run at him. His number was up, we all agreed that it would great to see him bleeding and broken and left to die. We waited in a line, he appeared over the bank. He was shocked to see us but braced himself for what was about to happen. The cry went up Charge. I ran at top speed barrelling into him, the next thing I was on the ground, he was beating me to a pulp and I was pinned under him. I shouted to my true mates to get on his back and hit him. I stopped because my eyes were closing and blood was running into my bruised mouth. He finally left what remained of me moaning and crying in the field. I crawled home to my Mum who patched me up and told me not to climb trees if this was what was going to happen. I found out later that when the cry went up to charge I went one way the other four went the other way. I learnt that you haven't got true friends in this life. I became a lone traveller. William Brooks never hit me again.

The second bully was again the same age but three times bigger than we were. We were all scared stiff of him. He took my six pence pocket money one day. He would rob the other lads of their sweets. He was a shit (well that's what he called us). One day once again he went for my pocket money. He hit me so I handed it over and he then proceeded to taunt me. Sticking his face close to mine, chanting hit me, hit me I was so scared but on this fateful day, why, how I did it I will never know. I pulled my arm back then drove it forward, his nose exploded, blood everywhere. I ran and to this day I don't understand how I did it, also why I didn't get into trouble. He never hit me again. Just a few weeks ago I was in the local Post Office and there stood my blooded friend. He had no idea who I was. I moved a little closer to him. Ooooooh yes, that's him he has a slight bend in his nose.

Mates, still you never find the true ones, that maybe you dreamed about in early life.

MY MARRIAGE OVER

My marriage over, it was sometimes my good fortune, maybe not, to meet a lady or two. They proved always to be great times. They have fun, go anywhere, and if you were friends it was great. However if you became more, i.e. you slept together, made love together, oh they would seem to change. I can't do that. I won't do that. Why do you do that? Ooh that's far too dangerous, sit on a bike for miles no. Their main aim in life seemed be, to want to change the person they were with (ooh) so in love with me. My philosophy is why can't you be close, make love, have fun? I never want to own anyone, life is to share, never to own, fun is to share, never to own, because you give yourself to another you don't own them, don't try to own them, they are their own person. How many times have you heard, I don't know what the Wife would say, the Wife wouldn't have that. (Wrong) couldn't we share, I don't know what my Husband would say, my Husband wouldn't have that, my Husband wouldn't let me do that. Is it all an excuse? I don't know. I have no idea. Some seem to be saving themselves for the next life. Is this a trial run? You tell me. With good health one has this over whelming sense of freedom (this will never leave you.)

MY CHILDREN

My children did come on the back of my bike. My Daughter was the first one on my bike. We did local runs. One day we both fell off the bike, she was fine, but I wasn't. The thought of one of them hurting themselves was not easy. Good job she was wearing the right gear. My Sons did several continental trips with me. For us these were great times, we are pals always. My oldest Son was at the age of looking for girls when we did his first trip. We pulled into a campsite one evening. I was booking in and the Lady said, "Just find a place you like", so my Son went looking. All booked in I started the bike. I soon found my Son, he was pointing, so I pulled up there. To my surprise there were two very French Ladies sunning themselves. No clothes on to stifle the sun, so we camped there for a day or two. He did befriend them, but I have no idea how far his befriending went. My youngest Son, I am sure he fell in love a few times. Both my Sons are very good fisherman. My youngest would be happy to fish, so now and then we had a great fish supper. Where ever we went people loved them both. That was great for me and I am sure they loved it to.

NO MORE OF THAT, I AM A LONE TRAVELER.

Gosh they do miss out.

I CROSSED THE CHANNEL TRAVELING IN THE EARLY DAYS

Just a week away, I will just do a bit of Northern France. I slowly packed my bike, tent first, the children's Weetabix wonder world tent, a used sleeping bag, wrapped in a large plastic bag. An abundance of plastic bags became quite a thing in our household. It stopped when I got divorced (I found that odd). A little gas burner, cup, plate, spoon, knife and fork, one pair of trousers, two shirts, two pairs of pants (one on, one off) one pair of shoes and two clothes pegs. That was about it.

Days before my departure, the bike was packed, unpacked and packed again. My motorcycle gear consisted of an old leather jacket and trousers and boots.

With black plastic bin bags inside, it stopped the water getting to my feet. My boots were totally porous. I also included a plastic over suit. Two days before I was shitting myself (France). Ooh what have I done? I would agonise over leaving my now growing up children, but I knew I had to do it.

The morning arrived, I had no breakfast I couldn't stomach it. Saying goodbye to the Children and my Wife made me sad, not knowing at the time my marriage was approaching its end. So really I would not have had to worry if I had known, her future was already set.

I am not a goodbye person and can get quite upset. I pushed my bike to the gate, fired her up and was away. It was early so not many people were about. I motored on steadily this wonderful beamer was talking to me, (man and machine in harmony). I was heading for Weymouth. My thoughts were could I find the ferry? Hope I won't miss it. I was also listening to the engine, something I have had to live with over the years. The old ones always put up problems. It was years before I just trusted my bike and German engineering.

Well that's good the ferry signs started some way out, I was soon checked in and sat on the port. My passport was OK money stored (I had allowed myself £5 per day) fuel, food, and campsite. I was double shitting myself.

A few years later I arrived back at a port in France ready for the ferry home. A dear friend had taken her driving test and I was desperate to know how she had done. I had a tank full of petrol that's it, not a bean. I was talking to a couple on the Port. I told them about my friend, "well ring her", they said. "I can't I have no money". They said, "Ring her" and gave me 50p. She had passed. The couple that gave me the 50p said to one another how wonderful. A tank full of fuel and no money! They seemed turned on about that. I was unphased I had 20 tins of fish plus two bottles of wine in my panniers, so I could eat on the way home if I needed to. I had a bottle of water, so it was really no problem. When we went onto the ferry, they paid for my dinner. They weren't feeling sorry for me, just turned on to the way I travelled. Strange. Things have changed.

THE FERRY

Then something new happened to me, a couple walked up to me, saying, "I like your bike, where are you going camping then, are you on your own"? Well this is new to me (you have a bike and people talk to you, STRANGE but nice). My reply was "thank you, I have no plans as to where I am heading". Their response was "how wonderful"! "Well yes, I suppose it is". (No mates, just me) "Why you are brave". "Am I"? There it was. "We had a bike but we are a bit too old for it". Well then I did respond, "YOU ARE NEVER TO OLD". She said " John shall we get another bike"? He replied, "Well we could do dear". "Well I would love it", she said. I was a gasp with all this and I hadn't moved off the Port. A woman who wanted to travel on a bike, people who admired what I was doing, this is new to me. They wished me a good trip, exchanged addresses and off they went. I have found over the years that if you are on a bike people will talk to you, in a car they won't. I have made most of my friends because of my bike.

I had some insulation tape with me to put a little on the headlamp. It's the dipped headlight that goes the other way.

Oooooooooh they are loading, this was new I had been sent to the front of the queue and was first on. Up the ramp, take it steady the surface was very wet. I was OK I kept the shiny side up. I was directed to the side corner and given a rope to tie my bike to the side. This I did (about four times before feeling happy about it).

Right all done, check passport, money, this done again I made it to the Cafeteria carefully planning my route back to my bike. After many years of travelling the world on my bike I always treat my bike as my home. That always kept me positive and focused. I never left my bike for very long it was always close to me. Latterly my locks were better and an immobiliser helped me but I know if they wanted to steal it, it would take four people and a van, so this always made me vigilant.

PARKING MY BIKE

My parking too close to my tent was nearly a catastrophe. I was camped in the Dordogne and during the night there was a terrific storm. When I crawled out in the morning the bike was at an acute angle over my tent about to fall. The rain had softened the ground and the side stand was slowly sinking in the earth, slowly leaning more and more towards my tent. From them on I carried a small piece of wood for the stand to sit on and parked the bike just away from my tent. As I moved the bike away from my tent, I noticed the ground was washed away and there was a very large old door key. I soon had it packed and I still have it today.

ON THE FERRY

I found the Café and whoo look at this a cooked breakfast (on five pounds a day it doesn't take in breakfast as well) so I had one of my sandwiches and a cup of tea.

   I wandered around the boat and then sat down. I had a look at my map, planned a route thinking that looks OK so I will go that way. I believe I then fell asleep (not surprising as I had been strung up like a bow string while still trying to look in control). I must have been exhausted.

CHERBOURG FRANCE

I was awoken by an announcement that we were docking. Oooooooooooooh lord.

I found my way to my bike, donned my gear and untied my lady. Engines were starting, so I fired her up and sat waiting. I was waved forward into Cherbourg.

I have learnt a hard lesson over the years. Let the ass hole car drivers go. If you try and get out with them they hit you off your bike. This has happened to me many times even worst they get out to see if there is a mark on their car. True, and you are led on the floor alongside your bike, unable to pick it up anyway. That doesn't seem to matter. I strongly believe that before taking a car test people should do a course on motorcycling. To be honest, half of them never notice you are there.

BRITISH SNOBS

Another little ditty, I was pulling out from the petrol pumps somewhere in France. A car pulled straight across in front of me. I braked hard and stalled the engine. She flooded and wouldn't start, battery flat I needed a tow or push. I spotted an English Jaguar. I walked over and said would you give me a little tow or a push as my bike has flooded and won't start. His reply was in this cut glass accent "I am going to have coffee, I will help you later". "That's fine" I said, but as they walked away his Wife said in a very loud posh voice "YOUR NOT GOING TO HELP HIM ARE YOU DARLING"? Uh what a looser, right, so in my best French of which, I know very little, I asked this group if they would give me a push. Straight away they were all around me and within four meters my bike was running again. With great enthusiasm they sent me on my way.

FRANCE

Riding up the ramp (this is France) Cherbourg. OK you're on the wrong side of the road, go steady, and look for the signs. Well look at this, it's different. I was soon out of the town and heading south. My girl running well, I was so happy to be on my bike again. I was thinking to myself don't run on too late you will be very tired, so I motored on. I started singing, this routine continued over the many adventures I had, Pearl's A Singer, Big John, Hear The Whistle Blow, by who I don't know. With a crash helmet on you think instantly that your are a wonderful singer and with Pearl's A Singer I think I am nearly up to Elki Brooks standard.

My first long avenue of trees, how wonderful! I have always loved riding though them. This has stayed with me over the years. The quiet small villages with a Policeman hiding behind the village sign, they never caught me but it was close at times. St Lô, Mayenne Laval, I was then following the river Mayenne.

My next challenge was some shopping. I found a street with shops and some people. I parked in the street and proceeded to shop. Well a charcuterie, looking at this, what's that? How do they do that? Is that cooked or pickled? There was no Waitrose in the UK then, so can you imagine what I was looking at. My first purchase was water, a baguette and a very big pickled pigs trotter (I think), plus sausages for my evening meal. These did not look much like British sausages, (well they wouldn't you're in France), plus a bottle of the cheapest wine I have ever seen. It was many years later after many bad stomachs and headaches that I found out I had been drinking cooking wine. My shopping cost very little. I then walked across the road, making sure I could see my girl, and sat on the grass outside the Marie, and devoured this wonderful meal. Full, with the warm sun on me I lay back and soon fell asleep.

I awoke feeling refreshed. It was time to camp and I had seen a sign for camping on my way into the town, so following the signs I found my first camping municipal. There was only one other tent there. I found a pitch, parked my lady and proceeded to pitch my tent. The weather was nice so no need to worry, as the tent was a bit short, my feet stuck out one end and my head out the other end. I had painted it with some weather proofing stuff, but had not tested it.

MY FIRST FRENCH TOILET

I had heard stories about these toilets, also the urinals in towns where you just stand on the street having a pee, your upper torso exposed. You can pee and pass the time of day at the same time. How wonderful Uh! I then had a look at the toilets and had a bit of a shock, a hole with places to put your feet ooooohhh this is different. Well when in France do as the French do. What if you slipped? The showers were nice so I showered and went back to my tent. I started cooking my diner. I set up my little gas burner. Dinner this evening was sausage and beans. This went down very well. Then I settled down with my map and planned my route for tomorrow. Nobody appeared at the other tent (strange) oh well. I locked my bike and settled in for the night. It was dry and warm, thank goodness. I was tired and I passed out.

Morning arrived and once again it was sunny. I needed the loo so I legged it over to the toilets. Ooooh yes it's these. Well ones biggest fear is you're going to slip. If you do, you are right in the shit (for want of a better word). All the ones I have had to visit seem to have never been cleaned. You don't ever have to look for them you just follow your nose.

With the sun out this always makes you feel good. I dropped my tent, packed my bike and was ready to go. I looked around to see how I should pay. At that moment a chap appeared relieving me of a very small amount of money, the campsite cheap or what? I think he wished me well "Like your bike". Well I think that's what he said.

I had no plans for breakfast. I fired up the big twin and was soon on my way, tramping south. I was looking at wonderful small villages. Hey look at this! It looked like a street market. Um let's have a look at this. I parked my girl there was interest in my bike before I got off, (this is new to me). I think I can live with it, well education or what? What's that they are cooking? Do they eat that? I could have bought a chicken for my dinner. The problem was I would have had to kill it and remove the feathers. I moved on. I did a little wine tasting on the way through the market. Should I get something for dinner? Well it's hot it could go off. I then came across a chap with a very small cooked gammon. Well I think that was what it was. It was cheap so that was diner (with beans) bliss! It was about lunchtime so I bought a cooked sausage with some sort of fried potatoes (it looked good) plus more water. I then wandered back to my bike to find a small group of people admiring her. I think they said they liked the bike but later I thought about it and maybe their interest could have been because I had my under pants pegged on the rear carrier (washed in the shower last night) oh well! A friend told me some years later that it was the under- pants they were looking at not my bike. Well I don't think underpants are that interesting (who is he)? Maybe they just liked a good laugh. Lunch once again was eaten in front of a magnificent building. I couldn't make out what they did there until a chap appeared in some sort of military dress and there's me parked on his lawn eating my lunch. As he walked by he passed the time of day (I think) and went on his way). He seemed like a nice chap. I lay back and went to sleep. I woke up feeling a little burnt, and it was now very warm.

THE FRIENDLY ENGLISH TRAVELLERS

Time to move on, so fire up the girl and on my way. I had a wonderful afternoon riding alongside a river. I found out later it was the Loire. Riding by the river I saw a campsite sign, another municipal and boy was it nice. An attractive lady was in this little hut by the gate (my French was camping s'il vous plait)? I was in. I could park up anywhere so I did. Afterwards a head appeared at a caravan window. "Hello lad would you like a cuppa"? "Well yes", this type of hospitality continued going ONTO A CAMP SITE (WITH A BIKE), so before doing anything I sat with my cuppa chatting to fellow travellers. They were on their two weeks holiday and had been doing their French trips for some years so nice. I thanked them for the tea, when off to sort myself out, then after an inspection of the toilet I was convinced I had made the right choice. It was very clean and also had a toilet sit down job, Great! Soon with my tent up I was tucking into dinner, um could be gammon or something like that (plus beans).

Showered I then sat outside my tent. There were quite a lot of people on this site. I was looking at my map deciding where to go tomorrow. Hey a good run would take me to the coast. OK that's what I will do. Bed, then some music started a few tents over from me. Music, off I go but I was standing at a distance. I was waved in and they were just travellers like me with two guitars. I sat down and was given a drink. I enjoyed the evening. Fortunately one lady spoke a little English. She had seen me arrive on my bike and asked me if I would take her for a ride the next day. I said I was sorry but I had my mind set on my route so I needed to move on in the morning. She came over to my tent and we sat and chatted. She sat on my bike and was full of it (this interest was new and quite a surprised to me) so my evening was very enjoyable. As it got dark I thanked her for her company. We parted with a kiss (well all the French do). She was Dutch. I didn't think this was just a good night kiss. Oh well nice while it lasted. I can't remember reading this in the instruction manual when I got the bike. My lady safe, it was bed for me, (hope it won't rain).

    I was up late I was supposed to be early. I prepared my bike for the days run. I thought get going and maybe I can get onto a beach. There was a lot of waving as I fired my lady up. It was always a bit sad to leave (nice people). I was away stopping at the first garage for fuel, then I tucked in and away.

MY BEACH

My beach

My lady was talking to me and within four hours I was nearing the coast, south of La Rochelle, north of Royan. The weather was great. I drifted until I saw a sign, which I think said sand dunes. I parked up. All the locks I had with me went on to the bike. I also chained her to a tree. After relieving myself of my leather gear, I followed a footpath through pines, the crickets were loud and the smell of the pines over powering. I rounded a corner and there was the sea. Oh what, how wonderful! I was alone, no one on the beach just me. Well off came my gear and I ran into the sea. This was my first taste of swimming with just my watch on. Boy was this exhilarating! (I hope there are no piranhas about). I stayed in until I felt I had cooled down, the walk through the pines had been hot work. I was so taken at the time with this coastline. On my future long trips across Europe I would try and make a stop here to rest my bum before my run north to the Ferry and home. One year I called in at my favourite beach, had a swim and led in the sun. I had been riding for about two weeks. I dropped off to sleep, some two hours later when I woke the sun was so warm I felt a bit uncomfortable around my one bum cheek. Well try looking at you bum, you can't, try looking on the side of a road in a bike mirror, it's not easy, you can't stop a passer-by and say hey have I got a blister on my bum? I couldn't get my head around enough to see, so it was sore for days. It must have been a big blister (well it felt like it). I put suntan cream on it, well that's all I had. Even in the mirrors in the shower block, I would just get my shorts down and I would hear someone coming. I just had to grin and bear it. Fortunately it was just above my sitting position on the bike so no discomfort there. But boy was it sore!

I SHARED MY BEACH

On two occasions I had to share my beach. I was not happy with this at all. On one occasion I was led out reading my book and three people walked down the beach I would say about 50 yards from me. It looked like a Mum, Dad and a Daughter of about 15 years old. They had no clothes on. I knew they were English, (how dare they use my beach). After their swim, they became brave and came with in 10 yards of me so for fun, I said excuse me have you the time please? They told me the time but were going around one another all up the beach. The adults I have no problem with, if they want to take their clothes off fine but not the young girl, when she is old enough she can then make her own decision on that sort of thing. I did embarrass them very much asking the time. What fun!

The second one to infiltrate my own private beach, some years later was at first most acceptable. Again after a long trip, I was resting my bum. From nowhere this beauty appeared on my beach. There was half a mile of beach each side of me but NO, she came within 10 feet of me, led down and got her book out. She said "hello", in I think Spanish. She was dark with a body second to none, a body you would die for. She was wearing nothing and to say that she was good looking was a gross understatement. I raised my eyes to the sky and said thank you lord. I am only a country lad, thank you thank you. I led there thinking how is this going to go? She was very intent on reading her book, but now and then gave me a nice smile, oh myself, who wants a book when they have this to look at? After an hour nothing, then out the corner of my eye I saw this dwarf with so much hair and three legs waddling along my beach. Yes life is cruel. He was waddling towards us (my dream was crumbling in front of me). Yes he flopped down beside her. She rolled over and kissed him, pooh no, this can't be but his third leg was getting in the way so maybe. I was hurt so I gathered my book and moved out of sight of my once short dream. Life can be hard.

SAINT SORIN

After finding this wonderful empty beach, I spent my day resting, swimming and writing my diary. This would always be my very special beach. Finally with evening drawing in, I thought I had better look for a campsite. Having seen a sign on the way in I headed in that direction. After putting my leather gear on (ooh hot or what) I followed the signs. This campsite was some way out of the town, quite rural really. Finally finding it just outside the village, I rode in. A very nice lady was in Reception and she was called Monique. She again was delighted to see a biker, asking me to join them the next evening for dinner. She laid food on for any one on the campsite, but you had to give her your order the night before. After booking in and setting up my tent, she came across with some chips, while I was having my meal. This was very much appreciated hence I have stayed there many times over the years. My plan was to stay two days then start moving north. I was the only English vehicle on the site, (that would change). I had a very good night's sleep, waking once again to a bright sunny morning. Having forgotten to check the toilets out, I found them to be first class and they had a sit down job (wonderful). Showered I was ready to face the day. I decided I would explore the area. I was camped next to a field of sunflowers, what a wonderful site, heads down in the morning, sun up and away they go, all looking the same way. Monique waved as I left the campsite. My dinner tonight came into mind what did I order? OK it was something with chips, (sounds good to me). I headed for the coast, running over a very long bridge, the river below and the fishermen coming and going.

MY FIRST OYSTERS

I saw some signs. I am not quite sure what they were selling. OK stop and have a look, I did. I parked my lady and walked across to this hut. OK GOT IT! oysters, so many of them and then I found out that I was in a big seafood area of France (should have read the book). Well with a lot of sign language I sampled six different varieties, with lemon, also a sauce, that was really good. You may ask how did I manage to get them down and to stay down. I have never had a problem with any seafood, so it was comparatively easy. So feeling happy with my oyster encounter, I moved on. On my next stop I came upon another market, again they were selling some wonderful local products, plus so much seafood. I bought some sausage thing with salad for my lunch, as time was moving on with all these stops. Well it's all so interesting. OK off to the beach. My afternoon was spent on my beach, just me my book and the solitude. I swam in the cool clear water. This is so wonderful. I fell asleep in the warm afternoon sun, bliss. Before leaving my beach I had one more swim and was thrown around by the waves that had grown in size and ferocity. This is the Atlantic after all.

OK I then gathered my bits and walked back to my lady, packed my kit and fired her up back to the camp-site. On arrival I found an English caravan parked next to my tent. Parking my bike I bid them a good evening. There was a very reluctant good evening back. Oh well they could be British snobs. It was a couple. The man seemed to be shielding his wife (what have they in mind)? Are they under the impression that you are going to jump on their Wife? This is quite normal behaviour and I have never worked it out. So I beetled around and got myself showered and picked my dinner up from Monique. I sat outside my tent and my new neighbours had the same plans but out came the table chairs and candelabra. Well that's nice, I found it a very entertaining evening just eating my dinner, reading my book and picking up bits of their conversation. He turned out to be the best looking chap she had ever seen and he himself had the biggest sex drive. This had arisen only since he had met her. Every woman envied her for her wonderful full figured body. I thought if they drink much more they will just go for it on the grass. I hoped they wouldn't knock the candelabra over. Time for bed, I turned it. They were quiet and my night was peaceful, morning came so soon.

  Slowly I did my ablutions, then fired my lady up and made for the beach. My neighbours had not surfaced, so firing my bike up gave them a call.

FOOD IS FRANCE

I had planned to get breakfast and lunch together. I found the local supermarket in Marennes, this is food shopping at its best. One baguette, 4 slices of salmon, 2 hot sausage rolls, French sausages, different but nice. That was breakfast. I sat outside at the cafe having a cup of tea (yuck), not English tea for sure. What do they do to it? It's just not English, which is because I am in France. I was trying to discreetly eat my sausage rolls. I just sat taking in the people passing by, some admiring my bike. OK the beach, then I noticed a poster advertising a market in Royan. I think I may do that first. It was quite a quick run to Royan, as I rolled into the town people were walking this way and that with their shopping bags. There was the market. I was able to park my bike next to one of the stalls, stowed my kit and set off. Well there was everything any one would ever need. The smells were wonderful. Pooh I had bought lunch and look at all this. There was a small antiques market as well. This I found very interesting and bought a nice little penknife quite old with no doubt a lot of history. This to go with the other thirty I had at home. The market was packing up, when I finally moved on with something else to go with my lunch, so now it was salmon and Roquefort cheese (well why not), plus a little salad.

   I fired my lady up and away. It was about three by the time I reached my beach and again it was just myself. I settled into my wonderful lunch. I opened my book then I fell asleep, having had a wonderful day. Sadly as I would have to start moving north tomorrow, I set off back walking through the pines, taking in the wonderful smells and the rattle of so many crickets. My lady was fine. I donned my gear and motored into Marrenees. I parked up and wandered into the bar. Just a glass of wine, oooh look at that, a small seafood platter, that's dinner. Out the window went my £5-00 per day. I took a seat outside and I sat for an hour with my wine and my wonderful meal. It was buzzing with people doing the same. Whether they were on the way home from work or on holiday like me I don't know. What a nice atmosphere. In one restaurant some year's later, muscles were cooked in front of me. They covered the muscles with pine needles and set light to them. After they had burnt out they brushed them off and served them, it was very very nice. I was hanging the day out but finally I made a move back to my canvas accommodation and a very quiet campsite.

My neighbours were still very full of themselves and still both the most wonderful person they had ever known (I wasn't supposed to hear that bit). She was wonderful, (the most wonderful sex he had ever experienced). Oh he's done it before then. He was so full of shit. I think he should have said the most wonderful love he has ever experienced. I think he slipped up. OK enough, bed for me (well maybe a bit envious) good night.

MOVING NORTH

After a blissful night I was up fairly early to map out and plan my route. Once again the morning was bright. Taking my time I broke camp, loading my bike, I was getting the hang of this. My plan for today was to run near to Cherbourg, camp for the night and catch the ferry in the morning. Packed, goodbyes to Monique, I was once again on the road and loving it. The R90S was talking to me. I set a good pace and by midday had covered two thirds of my days travelling. I found a great lunch stop (a hut with chips) food seems a big thing when you are in France. I think for me any country's food is a big part of my travels. I sat by the river with my chips and some cheese from yesterday. What more could anyone wish for? What could be better? I took a swim in the river it was very refreshing. I dried in the sun then I led back and fell asleep for about an hour, just bliss. Thinking this is freedom. This is something else. My bike became Miss Freedom one. OK away again. I then seemed to follow the river for miles, stopping to take a photo or two. I think I will camp by the river if possible this evening. Another hour and I was looking for a campsite. This was easy, I seemed to find so many campsites by the river. I went into the town and had a look. I picked up my evening meal and a bottle of wine. It was some time before I knew the difference between cooking wine and drinking wine, my stomach was telling me once again, but it wasn't until a lady explained it to me in a super market that I found out that having the very cheap stuff wasn't the way to go. Then I went back to the campsite.

A FRENCH LADY

The lady at the Reception said she had seen me in the town. Her name was Florence, rather English I thought, so we chatted as you do. I handed over my passport and after taking my details she said "I do evening meals if you needed to eat". My first though was how much? I said, "Some chips would be nice". Then she said, "Well chips and lamb is a few franks", so oooh well why not? She said "what time would you like your meal"? We agreed about seven thirty, a very early evening meal for France. This would give me time to shower, walk and plan my route for the next day.

Seven thirty arrived and I went to get my meal. She said, "Would you like to sit here"? Well again it was a lovely warm evening, so we sat together and chatted, really mostly about England, the weather there, the food there and what area I came from. She seemed very much alone, well there were no children or a man about. She did the campsite in the summer, and I think worked in a hotel in the winter. I enjoyed her company very much, also the very nice meal. How she cooked the lamb I have no idea but it was very much appreciated. Finally as the mosquitoes gathered momentum, they like eating my ankles, we said good night. I enjoyed my evening with her. I wished I could have stayed maybe another day but the ferry was booked. I hoped I would come this way again.

I wasn't up that early I think it was the bottle of wine we shared. Washed and shaved, I dropped my little tent again packing it all away. I fired my lady up and as I rode away there were waves from lots of campers (it was so nice) I didn't know them but they loved the bike. I stopped at Reception but Florence wasn't there. I was away.

I pushed on and my lady was talking to me. Once again it was the avenues of trees and me. Whoa up Police, fortunately I was within the speed limit, but they gave me a very hard and long look. They seem to always be just beyond the village sign so no time for slowing up (just look for the village signs and slow down). I was making good time, my lady giving that effortless power.

CHERBOURG I RETURN

Cherbourg, I was looking for the ferry signs, yes some way out, so I followed them (I had learnt) if there was no sign to go straight on. OOOH the Port, I was waved through Customs to the Ticket Office where there was a nice chap. We had a little chat. He asked what area I had been to. I soon loaded him with my travels. He said he was a biker himself. OK I had my line number, but on arrival I was waved to the front. Well what's that about? I had not been on the Port long when I was waved forward. OK steady up the ramp, it was dry so it felt OK. I parked my lady roping her to some girder. I wandered off to the Cafe for a cup of tea, also striking up a conversation with a couple that wanted to chat about my bike and travels. Their first question was "are you on your own"? "Well yes". "Don't you find that a bit lonely"? "Well no", (I though after last evening with Florence, no not a bit lonely). "Did you plan your route"? "Well no, I just looked at the map night or morning and decide I will go to that place". "Did you book your campsites"? "No". "Ooh I couldn't do that" they said. So it went on and on, I think they were trying to talk themselves into doing it or not doing it, which one I couldn't quite make up my mind. They had been to a Hotel and I think stayed there.

The ferry was under way. I looked back as I was leaving France, thinking to myself I will return, saying to myself you will return. Sad to leave but I was happy at the same time. I think I was glowing, full of myself, from my wonderful biking and also my last night in France, however did that happen?

I found a corner and feet up settled down for a pleasant slumber. It worked I slept. I think I had about three hours sleep waking to bright sunshine. I had a wander around the deck, clocking ferries and also quite a few small boats. Being an hour from the Port I supposed that they were day boats. Occasionally I did see a very serious sailing boat, meaning business, a busy crew with the boat in full sail.

Well there is land, I have returned. I stayed on the deck until they called to my bike. I found my way to my bike, (luck) untied her and was sat ready to go. Finally I was waved forward, up the ramp again very wet, I think it's from the water in the boat. Steel and bikes are not a good combination. I was careful up the ramp and away. Customs was OK. They just asked me where I had been. They didn't look in my panniers. Well they would have only found tinned fish, one of my loves and in France there were so many different types of canned fish. I only had 10 or 20 tins. It wasn't £5-00 that day.

I was away the weather still holding. I was tramping on. Keeping to my left, just enjoying my bike and looking forward to seeing my Children. The traffic was light and I was making good time. Just 15 miles from home my pace quickened. I think several reasons, my Children, and my delight in my first bike trip to France.

I arrived home to quite a reception, so nice. I sat and relayed my travels to them. As the years went by they all became travellers.

MY SECOND BIKE TRIP

My life went back to my Family, my Children and work. I soon settled down to my working life but the time would come when I would sit for a while and dream. What I had done was such a big achievement for me, and to do it on my bike was just wonderful.

As a boy if ever my Mother's Brother was mentioned she would cry. I didn't know why (having no understanding of the war) I didn't know. He was 17 years old and killed at Ypres during the First World War. Thinking of this I wondered if I could find any information on what had happened to him, also if there was a grave. My Mother never knew if there was a grave or really what had happened.

I wrote to the War Graves Commission and a few weeks later a letter arrived. It turned out that he was never found, but his name is on the Main gate at Ypres in Belgium, so a plan was forming.

I think I would like to go there, for my Mother who never got over his loss. It's very plain to me now but as a child I had no idea or cared.

OK I checked maps and the Motorcycle News for ferry crossings, I think Dover to Calais a five day trip, maybe camping just outside Dover, taking an early morning ferry then maybe a good days riding getting near to Ypres in Belgium. Camping during the night then on to find the Menin Gate and a good look around the area. Well this would be a trip for the autumn.

OUR FAMILY HOLIDAYS

So our good life went on. My holidays with the Children were mostly spent on the west coast of Wales, but first it was Durdle Door in North Devon. All loaded up we were off. Well it was quite a run for us but we reached a campsite towards evening. The car was unloaded, while the children explored the area. We pitched the tent and when all was done and children fed, it was time for a good night story and off to bed. That night we were washed out, the tent pole broke and we spent the rest of the night in the car. I remember well seeing the people sat in there caravans just looking at us not one of them offered us a cup of tea or any assistance. We packed up and off home. We then found a caravan to let in West Wales so off we went again. This was the start of many great holidays in West Wales. My Children I think loved it, my Wife didn't. I am not sure if it was the coast she didn't like or spending two weeks away from home. Knowing what I do now I think it was the latter. I love it to this day and whenever I can I go there just for couple of days, walking the cliff paths and just enjoying the wonderful Pembrokeshire coastline. I remember my wonderful trip to Alaska, with its mountains and rivers, just wonderful areas, but if ever I am asked which I feel is the best, my answer is always Pembrokeshire.

MY NEXT ADVENTURE

The planning set in, OK I will go again but not for a while, but the planning never left me. My ex Mother- In-Law was quite interested in my trip and out of the blue one day she asked "could you find my Father"? "How do you mean"? She replied, "he was killed in the First World War and we never knew what happened to him". Well this was news to me no one had ever said anything about this before.

So when I had time I wrote to the War Graves Commission. They came back with two names the same, so I needed a little more information, so back to Mother- In-Law for his Wife's name and last known address during his wartime service. Armed with this information I wrote again and back it came. He is buried in Fillievres a little village in Northern France, so that went on my list of places to visit.

Autumn was approaching well I think I can make a dash to the coast and to Ypres. My planning went ahead, first dates, then the ferry, a very cheap crossing with the Motorcycle News. I think it was something like £10-00. Out of Dover for the first time, quite a long ride down to get the ferry, but I think that would make the riding on the other side easier. OK that then done, sorting out my kit, the Weetabix wonder world tent had been replaced with one that was long enough to have your feet and head inside (BONUS) QUITE POSH REALLY and handy if it rained. The date seemed to be on me in no time. Once again my bike had been packed and repacked, and I thought it's OK.

The day came, was I fretting? Yes. I said my good byes and wheeled my bike to the front of the house (what happened to that mate who said he would like to come) (my Wife would have said NO AGAIN) oooh get on with it!

I was making good time, pulling in only for fuel and my sandwiches. I was about 40 miles from Dover when another biker appeared behind me. He followed quite close for some time and as I approached the services he passed me and indicated that I should follow him. His pillion also giving me hand gestures to followed his lead and waved for me to follow them. I went straight on (strange that). Just out of Dover I started looking for a Bed and Breakfast, well in no time I found a row of houses and only one didn't have a Bed and Breakfast sign up. I soon had my bike parked in a back yard informing the lady that I was catching an early morning ferry. "No problem" she said. "Would you like breakfast? "No I didn't think so", (good decision). After stowing my gear I showered then walked to the local for what I considered a well-earned pint. I had my biking jacket on so was quickly engaged in conversation with the locals. They seem most interested in my visit to the Menin gate. One chap said he had been there and found it very interesting but also very sad. I had just one pint and then went off back to my digs for a night's sleep.

I woke about five thirty, was soon shaved and showered and fixing my panniers to my bike. I had washed my underpants in the shower so I pinned them to my carrier to dry out during the day. I would never be caught out with dirty knickers.

I was away and running along the coast road with the sea to my right. I was soon running onto the Port. Lord Customs, (thinking don't unpack my bike) they did! Where was I from? Where was I going? They had the lot on the floor. When they were satisfied they said OK. No attempt was made to repack it. I didn't want them to anyway. Oh just stop moaning and get on with it.

I did and was soon checked in and again sent to the front of the queue of cars. No bikes just me. I was waved forward. I crept onto the ferry over the wet metal plates. A Crew Member beckoned me to a corner gave me a bit of rope, so I got on with tying my lady to the bulkhead. I was busy doing this while noisy cars and lorry came on.

MY BIKER FRIENDS

Well that done, I looked behind me and there were the two people who had been following me yesterday. I shouted "hello" and I think I got one back. The lady came over to me. She said "can we go with you to the stairs"? I said, "Yes of course". So after he had roped his bike up three times (no change there) we found the stairs and made our way to the upper decks. You could at last hear yourself speak. "I am going to the Café", "that sounds good" he replied. I got my full English breakfast and made it to a table by a window. I could then see when we were moving.

My new friend's lady appeared with her breakfast. She asked me if I could help her Husband out as it was their first trip to the Continent and he wasn't sure what to expect. I was happy to share the little knowledge I had with them. Well he was jumpy. I really don't think he enjoyed his breakfast.

They weren't going far just into Normandy. I think he was hoping I was going the same way. We chatted through road signs, (if you don't see one go straight on). "How did I get on riding on the wrong side of the road"? "Well think your right hand is near the curb (throttle hand), traffic lights and asking for fuel". He didn't like the metal plate riding on and off the ship. How did I get on with it? I was shitting myself. "no I don't like it either". Lord he is greener than me. Well I think he was a little happier.

He asked, "Where are you staying tonight"? "Well I don't know" (oh he couldn't deal with that one) apparently, they had each night booked. Now this I couldn't do, you can't change you route or plans. No I like it as I am. We then headed off to the lounge. I put my feet up with him still chatting. I did feel sorry that I didn't go into the services last night when they signalled me to. I think it would have helped them, but you always look at the bad side, maybe this maybe that. I dropped off to sleep to be woken up to the announcement will all drivers re-join their vehicles. My friends had gone, their bike was there but I didn't know where they were. I was sat on my bike and then they arrived saying "oh dear we couldn't find the right stairs". They were soon on their bike. We said our farewells with a wave. As I was waved forward, they followed me very closely. It was easy straight through Customs and away. They followed me for some time then I turned towards St-Omar waving. I pushed my lady on and in no time I was seeing signs for the Belgium border. That's quick, oh well. I crossed the border near Bailleul heading for Leper Ypres. My plans were to camp near and visit the next day, but having made such good time, I decided that I would visit today.

HOW SAD

The Menin Gate

Running into the town it was hard to imagine what had taken place here, but the hundreds of graves gave you no time to forget. In what looked like the main street in the town I pulled in and asked some people could the direct me to the Menin Gate. They said, "Go straight on, you can't miss it". Not far down the road, yes there it was. I really can't say how I felt, not having known him, just seeing my Mother when he was mentioned and how upset she always was. I pulled over at a Cafe and parked my bike. I think I needed a cuppa so I sat on the street with a drink and a thousand and one things passed through my mind. It was making no sense so I finished my drink and walked to the Menin Gate. I walked up the steps and it was quite easy to find as it was in alphabetical order. There it was. I sat on the steps looking and thinking. I took a few photos. That was it really, it's just all so terribly sad. Why you are asking yourself, it never stops, it's going on today all over the world. Why?

I left the Menin Gate and walked up the street and saw a War Museum so in I went. I saw guns, ammunition, bombs and machine guns. This is what he was firing when he was blown to bits. Enough is enough.

THE BORDER

Back to my trusty stead I fired her up and away. I really had had enough so I was running across the country with intention of crossing into France this evening. On my way I stopped to look at a few Cemeteries. Finally saying look I think you have achieved what you came for, I pushed on leaving the Cemeteries behind at the same time running through some wonderful countryside. Near the border I stopped for a sandwich and fuel. On again, after consulting my map it was 50k to the border crossing. I needed to be pushing on. My lady was talking to me. I buzzed up to the border where two guards were in waiting . They asked where had I been and where was I going? They asked for my passport. This done I was on my way. French Customs just waved me through. As I crossed the border it started to rain, not light rain it was throwing it down, stuff the camping. The first town I came to, was looking a bit run-down. I was looking for a Bed and Breakfast and there on the left, I pulled up at the side of the house, to be greeted by a lady in the backyard. I asked for a room and she said they were closed for painting, the French painting, not something I had seen or heard about. I was under the impression paint had not got across the channel. It was then pegging it down and I think she felt sorry for me. "Well you can have a room but I will have to make the bed up". Great I had no problem with that. She pointed to garage type place, well a roof on stilts and not looking in very good condition. Well it was safe and out of the rain. I parked up, took my over suit off and hung it up. I looked around for the lady who had taken off to make the bed up I think. All I could see was rickety old stairs running up to the first floor. So I thought that's not it, it looked about ready to fall down, as does everything else around here. I sat down and waited and yes after about 15 minutes she appeared running down the stairs. She beckoned me over. My thoughts were it's never going to take both of us. It did and up we went. Well how pleasantly surprised can you be, my room was very basic, but clean and the sheets on the bed were whiter than white, they almost looked starched.

She was leaving the room saying I could have breakfast if I wanted. I said, "Yes if possible". I paid for my room and she was gone. I hunted around for the toilet, and found it along the Landing. There was no shower or bath that I could find but a wash hand basin in the room, which did me fine. After a wash and brush up, I locked my room and wobbled down the rickety back stairs into the street. Well I know most places look a dump in the rain, but this I think was a very unkempt place. I found a Bar open and ordered a sandwich, some sort of pate thing. It was so nice I asked for a second one. My Uncle was killed at the age of 16. He had put his age on, I wrote up my notes on today, I gave up on the details, that was enough. After a couple of glasses of wine, I wandered back to my clean room, the town seemed much run down. BUT never fear I had a nice bed for the night.

Waking quite late, what a wonderful comfortable bed. I had a wash and shave, listening for the lady with the breakfast. Not a sound, so after packing my gear I wandered out. Oh, on the landing was a little table with breakfast hot water in a Thermos. Well I hadn't heard her put this here. I tucked into a breakfast of croissant, sliced meat, cheese, and tea, no milk, oh well it's hot.

Breakfast was leisurely gazing out the back window at my bike. The sun was shining so everything looked as nice as it could. It was all a bit of a dump, and running through my head was my adventures of yesterday as well as planning my route for today. My direction today would be Cambrai. I wrote out my route and put it in a clear plastic bag and taped it to my tank.

Breakfast over I gathered my things and was off down the very rickety stair. I made it to the ground without it collapsing. I loaded my bike, still no one around so I fired her up and was away. My route was mostly

A roads, it was dry and I was making good time. I was running through a very rural area, when I spotted a chap just stood by his bike.

A FELLOW TRAVELLER

I pulled in and he indicated that he had run out of petrol. Well I had a pipe but nothing to put the petrol into because his bike was about the same height as mine. He went one way walking on the verge and I went the other. There was soon a shout as he had found a bottle. In no time we had a bottle full and his bike was soon running again. I think he had some way to go from what he had indicated on his map Germany I think, but he had just forgotten to refuel. I think he will remember next time. He offered me money, No was my answer. It's sad if you can't help a fellow biker. We were on our way. I followed him to the next Garage and with a wave pushed on. He was the first biker I had seen loaded up, so a fellow traveller It felt good.

THE FRENCH STREET MARKETS

The next town I came to was very busy. Ooh another street market. Well it's a must, and lunch was in the air as well. This market was very interesting, if I had wanted some ducks, rabbits, chickens, it was all there. Also there was local produce. After a good wander around I came out with bread, cheese, and a pickled pigs trotter, I was living like a king, all for very little money. Back to my lady my lunch stowed, I was away and looking for maybe a nice park or riverside, from my map. I knew there was a river not too far away, I pushed on for about 20k and yes I was crossing the river. So many nice places to park up, I saw a lane to left (not knowing then I would be eating out) I went to the Reception.

OUT OF THE BLUE

The lady who was in Reception, well nice or what? Her English was very good and we seemed to hit it off straight away. I was chatting to her for quite some time. She was very interested in my travels (I didn't tell her I had not done many bike trip to France). Finally I booked in. Right the toilets and showers looked at. OK I parked up and I noticed ooh they have canoes, well that's out of the question my five pounds wouldn't stretch to canoe hire. Well I could enquire. I went back to my very chatty lady. "How much to hire a canoe? She said so many francs, too many francs for me. I said "sorry" and she then said "I was going on the river this evening would you like to share with me". Half price, great a good businesswoman we arranged a time. OK what shall I bring? "Have you any wine"? "Yes I just got a bottle". "OK bring a bottle", she said. She would bring the dinner. Well whoopee this is great. WHAT this never happen to me in England (West Country boy on tour)! Great. So off back to my bike I then put my tent up and sorted out my ferry ticket and my route for the morning. I taped my route to the tank, all done kit stored. Passport again, what should I do with it? I found another hiding place. I couldn't take it in a canoe. I was more than a bit thrilled about my canoe trip, so off to Reception and Veronique was ready. It was such a wonderful evening, so warm. I asked who would take over the Reception and she replied that her Mum. OK we were both in shorts and tee shirts. We carried our red canoe to the river. She was in charge knowing the river very well (well that's what she told me). I was familiar with canoeing, but was happy to let her lead. She dropped our bags into the canoe and we were away. Heading up stream the currant was quite strong so we both dug in. We said very little just working at the river, every now and then she would shout and I would look and she would be smiling. I think she was pleased that I knew how to paddle the canoe. I think we had been paddling for about an hour, when we took a left turn into a narrow tributary. Not having to work so hard we had more time to look around and chat (I hope she knows where she is going). Within ten minutes the river widened again into a white sandy beach, wow, she took the canoe straight into the sand. What an idyllic place, we sat in the canoe and we chatted away, she was a single Mum, so worked and lived at the campsite with her Daughter and her Mum, who was a great baby sitter. We exchanged notes and a little more about our lives. She was very interesting and had many plans for the future. We climbed out of our canoe and sat on the little beach, this was blissful. "Swim" she said, "why not"? I was pulling my tee shirt off, she then proceeded to take the small amount of clothes she had on off. She looked around at me, "OK" she said. "Yes great". Well wow! (West Country boy on tour) she didn't bat an eyelid, so when in Rome do as the Romans do. I had read about brief encounters like this but um. So in we went, it was warm. We swam to the other bank, fooled around, chased one another, and just had fun. She said that if we swam just a little way in that direction there was a log we could dive off. Well I wasn't that keen, I had never liked jumping of diving boards, but well go for it, rounding the bend, well how idyllic is this, with clear blue water the log was waiting for us. I got the feeling she had done this before. I asked how often did she come here? She said all the time it's my bolthole. Veronique was out, up on the log and shouting to me come on, so when in France do as the French do, up onto the log and in. The water was quite deep, so clear and warm (good job it was) so we were diving to the bottom and meeting up, our swim was becoming very tactile, a great deal of fun. We surface in one another's arms both enjoying our fun, nothing else mattered only us, very gently, the warm water lapping around us. We lay in the shallow waters of the beach, finally lying on our beach. I was thinking this only happen on films, looking around for the camera.

WHAT AM I DOING? I didn't read this in the handbook, this biking.

Race you back, we did and there was quite a fight as we neared our beach. She beat me back, we chatted away. She was telling me her dreams of travelling the world, but her Daughter had come along so this curtailed her dreams a bit. She still had dreams but her dream was her Daughter.

Out came the wine, but no corkscrew, my penknife soon did the trick. She had two wine glasses, well I was in France, so we sunned ourselves, drinking the wine and just enjoying our newfound friendship. The sun started to go down. I said "we could have a fire on our beach". No need to ask her twice, she swam while I gathered wood and got the fire going. This is bliss I was saying to myself. She was beckoning me to swim again, she looked so relaxed, I walked towards her, flopping into the river, we were moving from the river to the beach and back again. Has this day got to end? Oh boy if this is touring I am coming again. There is more to this biking than you think.

We sat, having diner by our fire. We had some sort of pasta with seafood. It was very nice. I think anything would have been nice in that setting. We enjoyed a wonderful evening together one I will always remember. Is this real I was saying to myself. After the meal we curled up by the fire, really just to keep the mosquitoes and any other biting insects at bay, good job I put my shorts on, the light was fading before we moved off into the canoe and were away. She was right, downstream was fast, she steered the canoe from one side of the river to the other. When we were running over some shallow parts she hopped out, just fooling about. In no time we ran into the bank at the campsite, canoe stored, I thanked her so much for a wonderful evening. She said it was great. I kissed her good night and we lingered. She whispered, "Will you come this way again? I said "oh yes" (not knowing whether I would). She was gone. I wandered back to my lady and my canvas accommodation. What a wonderful day Sweet dreams (I did) oooh boy! There is more to this biking than meets the eye, I am thinking.

WAS IT A DREAM

I slept like a log, waking again to a wonderful sunny morning. The campsite was quiet, just a few people moving around. I crawled out and went for a shave and shower taking my time as my ferry was leaving after lunch.

Back to my tent I had cheese and a rather hard baguette for my breakfast. It went down well. I then took my tent down packed my bike. I was being observer by a few neighbours. Ready to go I walked to the Reception to say fair well to Veronique. I was told, by her Mother that she was not at home (well I think that's what she said). Oh feeling a bit sad I walked back to my lady, I fired her up, heads turned, I looked up and people were waving to me as I left the campsite. This I found in my future travelling happened so much. I was away. All day my thoughts went back to Veronique, will I ever see her again? I wonder why she wasn't there this morning. It would have upset me, so maybe not being there was right.

My lady took over my thoughts, I was thundering towards Calais. I so enjoyed my ride to the Port only stopping for fuel and a sandwich (food again).

FRIENDS FROM HOME

Onto the Port, once again I was waved to the front of the queue. So I am sat there taking in all around me and also thinking of my evening. Then I heard my name, looking around I saw two people I had known for many years. They were returning from their holiday. We were still chatting when they called us for boarding. My friends legged it back to their car as I was waved forward. I strapped my trusty stead to whatever was there and then made my way to the deck, bumping into my friends again. No sleep today.

We chatted away. They had been to their house in Lot for their summer holidays. I know he would love to have been riding his bike but stocking their house with things and furniture was curtailing his riding for a while. He had always been a professional rider, someone to admire, some years later they were more than friends to me, when I needed true friends.

It seemed no time and I was back with my bike again, giving them a wave I was away. I made good time but the light was fading, as I turned left from London heading for the West Country. It was very dark as I approached home, but I was glad to be back. An empty house, as my youngest Son was staying with his Girlfriend. I have never got used to an empty house on my return but I can live with it, one has to.

MY DUTCH FRIEND

I have a friend I met many years ago. I am now writing about him and his lady at that time, but I could only find a very few notes, in the diary. I wrote to John asking for any information as to the place we first met.

This is the letter from John my friend. I have changed nothing; this is how he wrote it.

I tortured my brain about our first meeting in the Alps but it's really hard to remember details. All I remember is myself and Margot sitting in front of our tent drinking a cup of tea and hearing the beautiful sound off a beamer (R 90 S) climbing and conquering the Col d'Iseran. You passed by the campsite but in a while you came back and entered the campsite. That's when you saw my beautiful black and white old lady, R60/6, Handsome Youngman and his lady in front of the tent.

You stopped and parked next to us. A very pleasant and warm meeting followed. You built your tent and from then on we were stuck with a very nice British Gentleman, (farting his way through France). Margot and I went out for dinner and we agreed when we come back we would drink a bottle of wine together. However, when we came back you were sleeping already. We drank the wine next day then we parted on our way for our adventure through France. The next day or two days later, I stopped at a petrol station to fill up my old lady (the beamer, not Margot) and unbelievable the nice and charming Englishman was filling up also at the same station. We had a nice chat and exchanged our addresses. There we go. That was the beginning of a friendship and lots of adventures together (sliding through sheep shit, drinking rum and being sick for a week, taking out German families on skis etc. etc. etc.). Now 25 years later, still going strong. Hope to meet again soon.

Love

John.

The Alps

My memory of meeting John and Margot was similar to his account. I rode passed a very large dam. There was a drawing on the face of the dam. I stopped and took pictures, then motored on. I was drifting, knowing it was time to look for a campsite. There was a sign, follow that I thought. This is a very nice area oooh looks like a nice campsite. I spotted another bike on the site but as always drifted into the village to have a look around. Yes I think this will be fine, turning I headed back to the campsite. I booked in and had a look at the showers. OK, I then saw the biker so I decided to park up next to him. He seemed quite happy about that, they both greeted me warmly. We chatted about normal things, our homeland but more importantly bikes. His was a 600cc BMW, a nice looking bike but two up and all that gear, quite a lot of work for it. During our conversation I was putting up my tent and sorting my gear. I also always gave my bike the once over as I had been running all day through the mountains. My bike was my home my friend, my company. It was also nice to chat to fellow travellers.

All set up I took out my boy's folding fishing rod and off to the river, maybe this time I would catch one. (I want be fisherman). It was a great spot to drown some worms so I was quite happy to sit and enjoy the scenery. I came away ready for diner but it wasn't fish, (well at lease I looked the part).

Back at my tent, it was meatballs and beans for diner (one day, one day it will be fish). My friends had disappeared, I think into the town for diner. Finishing up I headed to the toilet block and did my washing up. I took a shower, then bed, no bedroll again onto the ground sheet. This was the Alps and the cold was striking through the thin ground sheet. (Not a lot of good).

COLD THIS MUST CHANGE

The Flying Dutchman

My night's sleep was good but a little cold, I went to bed with my clothes on that helped, but I was going to have to do something, a mattress of some sort.

Crawling out of my tent, I had decided that a good cooked breakfast was the thing to do. While I was cooking away my new Dutch friend walked by. He took one look and quickened his step. Some years later he said that the sight of a fried breakfast made him feel sick. Strange that.

We chatted after breakfast, promising to keep in touch, well maybe. Our chats went well into the morning, in no hurry I packed my tent about mid-day. Finally saying goodbye to my Dutch friend I was away.

I sent my sights on Chamonix, taking a very scenic route. After about two hours I pulled into a garage for fuel. Little did I know that at that garage, low and behold were my Dutch friends. Well that's it friends for life. The second farewell was sad but I must now push on.

I rolled into Chamonix and mount Blanc was towering above me. Well what a sight! Mont Blanc or Monte Bianco both meaning White Mountain is the highest mountain in the Alps. It rises to 4,810m above sea level. At the same time I was keeping a look out for a campsite sign, there it is.

MORE BEANS

I also found a shop. The food shopping I found most fascinating, today I am in the same country but different shops, wonderful. Oh well it was some sort of beans and sausage again, but it was different.

    Delighted with the weather, the place, the food, I was on my bike and onto the campsite. The site was quite large, I booked in but the chap didn't speak a bit of English. Never mind I had a place to stay. I picked up from the campsite's office some leaflets on what to look at tomorrow. I had a look at the toilets fine also the showers were hot. I found a nice pitch and soon had my tent up. I then tried the showers and well they were very warm and very clean. Feeling good I took the long way back to my tent. Again there were so many different tents. I was particularly interested in the Igloo type tent. I saw one with a storage area on the back and it seemed to me a great place for your bike gear. I think this type of tent would be my next purchase, after a bedroll. I loved the different colours of the many tents.

MY ROUTE WAS SET

I stumbled upon a cyclist. He was just putting his tent up. He was German but he spoke perfect English. He was saying he had been at the site as a young man and had ridden the high passes (this I had no idea about). I told him I was on a motorbike and did he think I could do the same route? "Yes" was his answer. "I am doing it again before I get too old" he said. He said, "Are you around tomorrow"? "Yes". "I will write the route out for you". I thanked him and wandered on.

MY YOUNG TRAVELLERS

Back at my canvas accommodation, I got my dinner on, but didn't open my wonderful cooking wine as two English lads walking by spotted my number plate. They had a good look at my bike and also gave me a beer, at the same time inviting me to join them for another that evening. They were in the next field so not far to go. I sat outside my tent, once again my dinner was wonderful, the sausage so different and the beans were in some kind of sauce that did it for me. I will go back to the shop tomorrow for another tin. Oh boy is this living! Heinz beans make you fart but these have brought farting into a new dimension. (Maybe I should give them a miss.) WHY?

All washed up, I set off to the next field, the young lads were pleased to see me and we chatted. Their story was that they had been catching trains. Their trip was discussed last week and on a shoestring they had set off, and arrived that day at Chamonix. After chatting I think a shoestring had been an understatement. I am saying, "Well how are you getting back to the UK"? I really don't think they had thought about this at all. After two more cans of beer, they said they thought they would have to hike. Well that's a plan. I did insist that I paid for the beer they had given me but they were having none of it. So I invited them to my tent for dinner the next evening. This they accepted. I bid them good night and wandered back to my tent. I locked up my faithful friend. I went to bed, taking my wee bottle. After the beer I know I will need it. I dislike walking across a campsite in the early hours so the bottle it is. I drifted off to sleep, dreaming of my newfound friends Dutch, German and English and also this wonderful shoestring food and wonderful weather. Here I am at Mont Blanc. What more could anyone want or dream of? Dreams sweet Dreams.

MONT BLANC

When I awoke I think the birds had long sang their morning song, I led there the sun streaming through a small hole in my tent, (bliss).

After my wonderful hot, very hot shower, I made a brew and ate my cheese and bread from yesterday. The cheese had heated up a bit so was a little oily, the bread was just a tad hard, but I enjoyed it. I sat with my leaflets and a local map. I decided that I would take the cable car to the mountain opposite Mont Blanc and then walk back down. This would give me a great view of the mountain.

I set off, with my small pack, water and hoped to pick up a sandwich on the way. It was quite a walk but there was so much to see, I was happy. Finding the lift, I paid and waited for it to arrive. I think it was half way when I arrived so I was able to watch its progress. By the time it arrived there were quite a few people waiting, all nationalities. I found this in itself very interesting.

The lift arrived and away we went, the sun was so hot and the view magnificent. Ooooh hello we ran into the cloud and the temperature was dropping fast. Well that was a turn up for the book. On arrival we all stepped out of the cable car into thick cloud. I had no idea what way was down, but stuck to an English chap with a very attractive Japanese Wife/Girlfriend, who I think were doing the same route. Well it's down any way.

I stumbled my way along, it was very cold but I had my bike jacket on so I was OK. Finally after about an hour, I walked out of the cloud and there was Mont Blanc. Well not all of it, some of it, oh just look at that it's wonderful!

Also my friends were just in front of me. I think they were relieved to be in the sunlight once more. His Wife wasn't really dressed for mountain climbing. We had a few words and I continued my walk, I think I had some wonderful pictures. I do hope they come out.

I then turned off to the right, seeing some chaps hand gliding. I stood and watched them. They were taking people on this two-seated glider. It looked wonderful. I then sat going through the money I had, thinking maybe if I did a couple of long days on the bike, I could do away with two campsite fees and stop the wine for a couple of days. This would give me enough money to take a trip on the hand glider. OK that's it I will do it. As I walked towards the little hut to pay a glider launched, it went out, a cross wind caught it and smacked it back into the mountain. Pooh that's it not for me. My money stored back in my wallet, I stopped to see if the chaps were OK then headed back to the descending path.

After a short walk I stumbled on the couple again, they were having a picnic. I stopped to relay my story of the hand glider, at the same time being offered a drink and to share their sandwiches. We sat and chatted. They were on their honeymoon. They had been married for two years but had not been able to get away until now. They were very nice. From what they said this was their first adventure together. They were interested in my adventure as they both were keen cyclists. They said they would take their bikes on their next adventure. I think they were thinking well as he is on his motorbike, we could do it on our bikes. Why not, I thanked them, this meeting had been a pleasure and I was soon on my way.

My next meeting was a little interesting but also intriguing. I met this chap walking up (fool). He asked me how far it was to the top. I replied that the cloud was very thick. Having said that it did seem to be clearing. He had some sort of uniform on but I had no idea what it was. Anyway we chatted and it turned out he was a very high-ranking Jewish Officer, just taking a day off from some high-powered conference. He told me quite a bit but nothing that I could piece together, so it was a lot of information leading to nothing.

He was quite fascinated with my bike trip and said it was always something he would love to do. Could I keep in touch, he gave me his card and we did keep in touch for some time. I also shared one of his sandwiches with him. I am thinking £5-00 a day with additions, so many sandwiches on one walk. I hadn't produced one. I started to wonder whether I looked under nourished. People keep offering me food. West Country boy on tour, that wasn't in the handbook. Well maybe I missed it.

Once again we said farewell he gave me the most genuine handshake I think I have ever had. I liked him very much and said, "Keep yourself and your family safe".

MY RAIN COAT

I was on my way once more. Ooh what's this, black clouds were appearing, soon down came the rain, this I was prepared for. I had unpacked some light fittings for my work some time ago. They had come in wonderful plastic bags. These I had saved. I had cut a hole for my head to go through, so I whipped it out my bag. On it went and apart from my soaking hat I was dry, quite a sight, but it worked. The heavens opened but I was dry ish. No one looked because they were all very wet, for myself I was dry.

As I neared the town the rain stopped, the sun appeared, my plastic bag was removed and stowed away in my bag ready for the next time.

I shopped, got treble sausages and beans for my dinner with the lads. No wine tonight as I didn't think my stomach could take much more of it (cooking wine), no wonder it was so cheap.

On my way back to my tent I stopped to see my German friend. He handed me my route for tomorrow. I said "do you think you will make it ok"? "Ooh yes, I cycle a great deal, it will be no problem". Thanking him I wished him a great ride. I wandered back to my canvas comfort.

I was a little concerned about my tent it wasn't the best but I found on inspection that it was OK, just a little water in one corner.

After my shower, I set to with preparations for the boy's meal, not much to do really. I only had one fork, one knife and one spoon, my little frying pan and one saucepan. I hope the boys have their own equipment. I had some doubt about that having talked to them.

Their names were John and Kevin. Kevin appeared asking what time diner was. It was ready so I asked him to bring their own plates and a fork. What appeared a little later were two paper plates and plastic forks, well that will work. They came over with six cans. I got the sausages cooked hoping they would keep warm I did the beans, well with the bread and beer it was a good meal, one to be remembered. The boys were doing a walk the next day to the lower part of Mont Blanc. I said I hope you are prepared for the cold. I described what it was like above the cloud today it was cold. We all enjoyed our evening I admired them. They had nothing and really didn't seem to mind. I told them I was leaving tomorrow taking the route the German chap had given me. We were not late saying our goodbyes I turned in, hoping it wouldn't rain.

THE ALPS

My canvas accommodation

My early start turned out to be a late start. I woke to the sun streaming into my tent, as the front zip was half way down. How lovely I just lay there just enjoying this wonderful place and my wonderful adventure. OK come on get up. This I did, I decided I am late so be late, take your time.

I had a cheese sandwich and a cup of tea. I showered then dropped my tent. I was loading my bike when John came up to me saying he had over slept and Kevin had taken off on the walk without him. He didn't know what to do. I said did anyone see him go? He said the chap in the next tent said he went out about six. I said "look you're not going to catch up or find him today so do something else". He seemed pleased with that and away he went. Strange why didn't he wake him?

My route planned and my bike loaded I was away to a few waves and horns blowing as I left the site. I was heading for Val d'Isere. My lady soon warmed up and we were eating up the miles then slowing down. This is just a wonderful twisting road, climbing, I am riding by the seat of my pants. So steep I am finding it very hard to keep the shiny side up on my bike, some corners if you can call them that I was footing my bike around the corners. On my journey I failed to see one cyclist walking with his bike. They had to be fit. Also what amazed me was the speed they were descending at I was over taken so many times by cyclists. I think my full panniers and my pack on the back of the bike wasn't helping to get around the air pin bends. I was so enjoying this.

I somehow don't think that I will be sticking to the route I was given. I think I will follow my nose. The next two days I took roads, tracks and dead end roads but why not, the scenery, the mountains and the valleys were just something else. Some roads were long weaving through valleys, the mountains towering above me. Some of the mountain climbs were steep very twisty and gravely. Some off road tracks were rideable, but sometimes it was best to turn around. My thoughts were if I go down there, could I get back? If I drop the bike there is no way I could pick the bike up and so my day continued. Lunch was a roadside van, just a great place to have lunch. The weather was great. I lay back in the sunshine and dosed for an hour, Bliss!

The wonderful Alps

On the move once again there were very few motorcycles on the road but again a great many cyclist. Late afternoon I seemed to be heading towards Grenoble, I found a campsite at Le Verger a nice quiet site. No office so I just found a nice pitch, unloaded my bike, put my tent up. I had been so busy enjoying myself I had forgotten dinner. It was no problem the shops were 5 minutes away, so tent up, I walked into the town where I saw a nice bar. Once again I sat watching the world go by having a nice cool beer and trying to take in what I had seen today. I had taken quite a few pictures so hopefully they would come out.

Off again to the supermarket, shall I have sausages again? Well they looked different, so once again sausages, but no beans tonight. I had potatoes um should be nice.

I walked back to the campsite and had my shower. I cooked my dinner, very enjoyable with the potatoes. I sat with my map for a while, but gave up, thinking just head south and see what comes up, so a compass job tomorrow. The man came by for the campsite fee, again very reasonable. I turned in.

I awoke early, the sun beaming in once again but it had been very cold. I will have to get a bedroll of some sort as the cold was striking up though my ground sheet. I had a shower trying to warm myself up. I then got my biked packed. I checked the oil, all OK. Right ready to go. Today in the mountains then tomorrow I will go south near the coast.

Being early on the road there were few people about as I motored on over mountains, deep valleys and breath taking scenery.

Early afternoon, I pulled over at a lake it was so hot but I had not really warmed up. I had seen the camping municipal so I decided to make camp early. I think I was suffering from my cold night. The site was Savines.

There was no office so again I found a pitch and set up camp. I sat for a while with my map and made a list of some of the places I had visited in the last few days. Col de l Iseran, Col de la bonette, the high pass 2,715 m some climb near the border with Italy, the Alpes

Maitimes, Alpes de Haute, Les Mees, Col de la Couillole 1678 m, this was a great climb but challenging, Tunnel du Maiquaires, L'alpe d'huez and Val d'Isere.

The Alps are one of the great mountain range systems of Europe stretching approximately 1,200 km across alpine countries from Austria and Slovenia in the east Switzerland and Lischtenstein.

Looking at my trusty steed, this is great. I finished my sandwich I had picked up earlier then settled down for the night. I just hope I will sleep warm.

THIS NOW HAS TO CHANGE

Wrong by the morning I had my entire bike gear on and was still cold. Decision made I have get a bed roll, this ground sheet is useless in the mountains, so after trying to get a hot shower (warm) I broke camp and dropped my site fee in the box by the gate. The first big town I come to I must sort my sleeping bag and bedroll out.

I have no idea what town I stopped at but it was quite large, I think I should find something here. I went to the Tourist Office. The lady spoke very good English. One street away was a big camping shop. I found the shop and I was directed to the sleeping bag area. My priority is warm and easy to carry on a bike. The cheaper Lilo types were far too big to carry on my bike. There was the perfect type, a thermal A rest. I pointed this one out to the shop assistant. I think because of my appearance cold and not shaved for a couple of days, he said "that's too expensive for you". Yes it was but if he had been feeling as cold at night as I had been. I think that he would have thought twice before saying that. I had to have it, also a warm sleeping bag. I tried to get some discount but he was having none of it. I finally left the shop with the two items plus a waterproof bag to pack them in. I had parked miss freedom outside a Café. I unpacked my bike and then repacked it, the new bag fitted in very well. Also there was not much extra weight. All done I went into the Café where I had been of great interest to all the cliental unpacking and repacking my bike, back out into the sun trying to warm up with a pot of hot tea. Admiring my new bag. I am sure this will solve my problem.

OLA -- JON

Moving south

Still cold, I decided to push on out of the mountains (joke) the day was warm but still I was cold. The riding was great and scenery spectacular. Nearing the area where I had decided to camp, I stopped at a charcuterie and bought some (I think) stewing beef and vegetables. Stew was on the menu this evening. I then rode south, in the direction of Guillaumes, getting near the village I started descending, steep, very twisty but what great fun. I saw a campsite so I went into the town to have a look. It seems nice so back to the campsite, ooh yes this will do. No one was in the office so I found a pitch parked my bike and legged it to the showers. If they weren't hot I was moving on. They were piping hot ooooh at last. I grabbed my wash bag and spent the next half hour in the shower, I came out rather pink but very warm ooooh thawed out at last. I wandered back to my bike and slowly pitched my tent ooooh. Then I laid my very new mattress down. Ooh it looks good. The sun was warm, I was warm, my bike was warm, what more could anyone want!

I then started my stew, not really like my Mum made but it will do. I cooked the beef in a sauce well a packet, this simmered away for an hour, and next I prepared the vegetables, beef off and vegetables on. Half an hour later, I kept the beef warm on the top of the vegetables saucepan.

Right it looks OK, smells OK. I tipped the vegetables into the frying pan with the beef and sauce. I then tucked in. What a meal, I was glowing. I leant back and took in the sun. Once again I was a little burnt when I woke up. I lay back thinking what a wonderful journey I was on.

I had camped quite early, so it looks like I will walk into the town to see what's going on and maybe a beer.

After locking my lady I headed for the town. Well what's all this, there were stalls, dancing, also food, food no, not after my stew. The food looked so good. But no, stew had changed my outlook on life my central heating was switched on, all down to stew.

I sat on the street with a beer, a cold beer. Who cares, I am warm and I need a cold beer.

A lady came across and sat at the next table. After a few looks I asked her if she spoke English (no). She then promptly left the table drink and all. Well all I asked her was did she speak English. Rather bemused by her departure I looked around for help. At that she returned with another lady, ooh lord what have I done. The second lady spoke to me in perfect English, well that's a relief.

She introduced herself as Ola, she was Russian, she then told me what all the celebrations were about, dating back hundreds of years, and this was for that and that was for this. All very interesting, we sat and chatted for a while. Then totally out of the blue she said, "I would like to take you to my house". Oooooh hang on a bit, what's this? She then said, "I have someone who would like to meet you".

I then quickly explained that I had almost frozen to death the last couple of nights, I had bought this wonderful mattress and needed to get back to it, but she was having none of it. "Please come with me"? Reluctantly I followed her. We walked up narrow alleyways, only about

100 yards from the bar we came to a building that looked rather like an old chapel. She opened the door and beckoned me forward at the same time shouting "Jon I have someone to meet you". There stood Jon, a very Welsh, Welsh man, how delightful, "great to meet you, do come in". Ola explained that I was on a motorbike and camped in the village. "Oh how wonderful, where have you been"? "Where are you going"? "Do have a drink". We chatted for an hour and at the same time Ola was cooking the dinner. "You must have dinner with us", ooh I groaned to myself how can I eat after the stew. I had no option I was staying for dinner, plus a drink and another one pooh, the wine was good (not my cooking wine) this was the real thing. I gave up and accepted everything they offered me.

It seems that they both ran an Art Gallery here in the summer months, in winter they went to their house on the coast, um nice, I don't think they are on £5.00 a day.

The evening progressed, 3 bottles of wine, a wonderful meal of seafood. It seemed to me none of us could see straight, could be the wine. I did enquire where the toilet was. "Just there on the right", I managed to get there and back, but had a funny suspicion that I was going to find it difficult to find my way back to the campsite. Returning from the toilet, I was informed that I was staying the night. "Thank you so much but I have to test out my new mattress". "No we insist", said Ola promptly taking my arm and leading me to this wonderful bedroom. "OK I give in". There is more to this biking than meets the eye. They left me to it and I crashed into bed. The urgency of my new mattress somehow seemed less urgent. Sweet dreams.

THE NICE PEOPLE ONE MEETS

I awoke to the sun streaming in through my window. I led there trying to think. Why I was in this wonderful bed? It soon clicked. Ha that's it, all was quiet. I went into the kitchen and I found paper and pen. I wrote a note, saying I had gone to the campsite and would be back in a couple of hours. I stepped out, down the alley and out into the square. There were a few people about, I believe cleaning up the square. As I walked along I was wondering why I didn't have a bad head, must be the good quality wine. (I had no idea). Back to my canvas accommodation I grabbed my wash bag and headed off for the showers. My mind was busy, how does this happen? I just met the lady, drinks, diner, and bed. Well that's nice.

Showered and cleaned up I went back to my bike. Slowly I packed my bike, packing the new mattress that had yet to be used.

There were more tents around me but I had been out for the night, so had not shared their evening but as I packed my bike there was quite a lot of interested smiles and studying. How I was going to get that lot on one bike? I did.

I fired my lady up. I left her to warm up while I paid. The office was still closed but at that a lady walked up and said she would hand the money in later (um she spoke good English). I walked back to the bike. More interest, I put my gear on and moved off so many waves. Full of my bike, and myself I was waving back, oops I nearly ran into the dustbin. BOYS!

I turned heading for the village and parked by the bar. The bar man said he would look after my bike, well I think that's what he said, I walked up to my friends. Ola was at the door ooh just in time for breakfast, ooooh lord more food. But food it was and very nice, very French, cooked meats, cheese, and fresh baguette plus a little fruit. I am thinking I won't eat for a week.

I so enjoyed being with them, hearing lots about their life. Ola had been a prisoner of the Germans, she told me quite a lot about it. Then suddenly she stood up and disappeared. Jon looked at me it always happens I wish she wouldn't talk about it. I went to go after her but he said to leave her, she will come back after a while. She did and we went to look at the gallery. They had some wonderful pictures, I believe all local artistes, also artists from the coastal area where they winter.

I felt I had to purchase something so I bought a post card, informing her at the same time it was all I could carry on the bike. (I had not told them about the £5-00 per day plus all this hospitality).

They wanted nothing from me. We all enjoyed our time together. It was nearing noon, we walked to my bike, they both sat on my bike took pictures. "Please come this way again". "Yes I will". Sadly, I have never returned, sadly it was Farewell.

THE PROVENCE

The lavender fields

The Provence is a region and historical province of South-Eastern France, this extends from the left bank of the Rhone River on the west to the Italian boarder on the east, this is bordered by the Mediterranean to the south. It is a wonderful experience to ride a bike through this area.

Heading out of the village, my direction west. My plan today was to ride out of the Provence, but after one hour of riding that changed, again, wonderful riding, and magnificent country. My trusty stead was talking to me. There was no stopping for lunch as I was stuffed. I just followed my nose stopping to take photos, trying to take in, the smells the lavender, fields and fields of lavender. I was so enjoying this ride. I had no idea as to where I was. The map had gone out the window. Late afternoon I saw a campsite sign, riding down the very narrow lane, oh there it was, surrounded by fields and fields of lavender. I just had to spend a night here, (tonight I would try out my new bed roll).

The site was very small. I booked in chatting to a chap who spoke some English. He said we do chips and small meals if I needed anything. I booked chicken and chips (in the Provence). I then found a pitch, put my tent up, took a shower. All done I took a walk (in the lavender) it seemed intoxicating, West Country boy on tour. I could stay here for a while, but I can't, look you're here, you're doing this, appreciate it. You're drunk on lavender. I dropped down onto the lavender, just spread out and led there, ooooh bliss! To add to the pleasure the evening was so warm, the weather had been so good. I was keeping my fingers crossed. I picked up my very French meal (chicken and chips). I sat eating my meal, also going over my map trying to pencil in places. I had also been planning my route for tomorrow. I must move west, the Tarn and onto the Dordogne.

I finally settled down for the night, my new bedroll was wonderful, I was warm and my hips weren't digging into the cold ground sheet. This was comfort at its best. Was it the bedroll that made me sleep so well or was I drunk on lavender? I have no idea. I slept.

THE TARN THE DORDOGNE

The Tarn

I was awoken to the wonderful sent of the lavender, just taking in how warm and how nice it was to feel the sun warming the canvas. I crawled out of my wonderful accommodation, wandered to the washroom and had a shave, now that was more like it, bike, bedroll, tent, clean-shaven, what more could a man want?

Breakfast was tea and beans, good job I don't share my tent with any one. I don't think we would be pals for long. I set to it, dropped my tent, and carefully loaded my bike, bedroll being stored in its new bag. Lord was I proud of my new bedroll.

I fired my lady up and was away, the plan was to ride hard today. I have to eat up some miles. I had some waves, as I left the site. This is a site I will never forget. (Lavender)

Slow riding, going West St-Audre-les Alpes, St Aubran, Volx, now I can start to move. Cadenet, Avignon, Ales, The Tarn Gorges, how wonderful. Now heading in the direction of Rodez, I only stopped for fuel, no food, as I was still feeling comfortably full. I wonder why?

A WONDERFUL STORM

It was late afternoon and I was running across the country. What wonderful scenery, the weather had been great but up ahead I could see some very dark clouds looming in front of me. I rode on (ever hopeful it would clear and I would miss it) no not the case. I stopped and put my over suit on OK I was ready for this. I quickly ran tape around the joints on my panniers. Well it started within half an hour it was just lashing it down (I will run out of it soon). I don't think so. The water was just rushing down the roads so it was not only coming down it was also coming up. OK decision made I made it to the next town. I walked dripping into the Tourist Information Centre dripping everywhere. I approached the lady, "I don't think I want to camp this evening", she laughed. "No I can understand how you feel".

She directed me to the Youth Hostel just across the road. She then said you just park over there and it's the door to the right. I said, "Can I park inside the building, have they a garage"? "No sorry, that's it". I just can't park on the street with all my gear on the bike. (Once again I am thinking my bike is my home when travelling). "How about a hotel"? "Yes" she said "but it's out of the town". "That's fine", so she rang them. "Yes they have rooms". She gave me the directions, which were quite straightforward. With many thanks I was on my way it was 5km, so just out of the town I found the tiny lane. OK up there for 1km on the left, got it, as I rode up the drive I saw a lady run from the front door to a small shed she was waving me in. Well she had cleared a space in the shed for my bike, just great, the lady at the Information Bureau must have told her I have a fussy English man who won't leave his bike out. We didn't talk as the rain was just thundering down and it had turned very cold, you couldn't hear a thing. She just pointed and ran back to the hotel. I parked my lady, took off my panniers and looked around. I think it is a tool shed normally but now a bike shed. Bike safe, I dashed to the Hotel, why I dashed I don't know I was wet through anyway. In I went and stood dripping in the small foyer. The lady was very welcoming and insisted that I looked at the rooms so dripping my way up the stairs, she opened several doors, but said "this is the nicest one". I said, "I would take that" and I dropped my panniers. She said she could dry my clothes by the boiler when I was ready. I thanked her very much, I was greatly relieved to have found somewhere out of this weather. I stood next to a four-poster bed in a puddle of water. OK get this wet stuff off.

Looking into my clothes pannier, well not much was dry in there. How had water got under that tape? I had to put on my shorts and a partly dry tee shirt after a very nice hot shower. I gathered my wet clothes and went to the Reception. Well it seemed very quiet, but as I approached the desk the lady appeared. She was very nice and very blond. I handed her my wet clothes she said "I will put it in the Boiler Room". I apologised for being in my shorts and tee shirt. I said, "It's the only dry things I have". We were then able to introduce ourselves she was Annia (a very attractive Annia). I handed her my passport and she told me the rates. Well it turned out to be 3 days biking allowance, but I wasn't going anywhere so I paid up. (THAT DID INCLUDE BREAKFAST)!

She asked, "Have you eaten"? I said "no". "Well the cooks not in tonight and you are the only visitor, but I could get you a sandwich", great so she said "I will give you a call when its ready". (Was I really hungry again)? I went back to my room and wrote my diary for the day. There was a tap at the door my sandwich was ready. She said, "It's in the small room next to Reception. I wandered down well sandwich (banquette) it was very, very French. She had lit the fire so it was very cosy.

She said, "Would you mind if I joined you"? "No" I said I was only too pleased to talk to someone who spoke such good English. I said, "Do eat with me", knowing it was far too much for me. The baguette, the ham I did recognised, the rest I had no idea, it was a cooked meats salad and various dip type things but it was good, plus a bottle of rose.

We sat and chatted she was very interested in my travels. Where had I been? Where was I going?

Then she started to tell me about her life and why she was in this rural Hotel in this part of the country. She had been married to a professional rugby player, married very young, things had not turned out very well and she had tried to leave him several times but, he had found her and back she had gone.

Finally with the backing of a good Solicitor and her parents she had gotten away and was now divorced from him. I judged her to be in her forties, she told me she was now so happy and had a very good friend who she had been staying with for two years. She was also divorced, she was happier than she had ever been.

Well as sleepy as I was this nice open fire and the conversation was keeping us awake. We chatted all evening going through both our lives, as the evening progress the conversation turned towards the more intimate part of our life's, we were deeply engrossed in one another. I think the wine played a part in this, we were warm and cosy, we lay on the sofa, it was so nice, some things always are, we both fell into one another. Suddenly the front hotel door opened with a loud creaking, Annia was up and out the door in a flash. Peeping out it was her boss who had called in to see if all was well. I thought more about had the roof leaked? It was still throwing it down, knowing my girl was safely in the warm shed I was happy. I sat for a while hoping my new friend would appear and after half an hour I made my way to my room. I though I would take another shower then go to bed. I heard the front door of the Hotel close and though well it looks like I am on my own for the night. I didn't hear my door open, my shower curtain went back, she held her hand out, I guided her into the shower nothing was said it was so nice. I shared my wonderful four-poster, oh boy!

I like this travelling, being free isn't that bad, there seems to be more to this biking than meets the eye. I must read my handbook yet again.

I awoke to the sun beaming in through the window, Annia wasn't there, and I didn't hear her go. She must have opened the curtains and left. I crawled out of bed the view from the window was panoramic. Well I didn't see any of this last night I had experienced Dordogne rain.

I looked out of my door my now dry clothes were on a table in the hall so Annia must have been busy this morning.

I showered once again well 3 days travelling money why not (I wonder if I left the door open) just have your shower and stop dreaming.

I then packed my panniers. I had everything ready to go. Breakfast was more or less like supper, very enjoyable, plus good English tea, my waitress this morning was the boss, who had called in last night. She was very nice, very French and we got through breakfast, with no English from me and very little French.

As I went outside with my gear and panniers, I looked around for someone (hoping to see Annia) but there was no one. It wasn't until I fired my lady up that the Manager appeared. She waved as I moved down the drive happy but a little sad. Annia really was happy.

I was once again heading first west then north. I was only a short way from the hotel when I saw her. She was with her friend arm in arm walking their dog. They both looked, they heard the sound of my engine I put my hand up and they both smiled and waved.

SIGHTS SET SAINT SORIN

I was on my way, my plan was to spend two day at my beach, then north to the Ferry. As I turned north onto the main roads, I was tramping on my lady eating up the miles. Brive, I turned west again then headed for Marennes. I was approaching Marennes by late afternoon my only stop had been fuel and a sandwich.

Marennes (Charente- Maritime) is a big seafood area Marennes oysters are exported all over the world. Charente Maritime has 460km of coast, wonderful beaches and some times wild seas. I was getting to know this area.

I stopped at a supermarket, got my dinner, and headed out of the town to my campsite, hoping it was still open. Yes there was Monique, both delighted to see one another again. She said, "Pitch your tent anywhere". No need to check the toilets, I know its fine. They have a sit down job, (bliss).

I was soon parked up, tent up and showered. I sat outside my tent writing up my last few days travelling. Last night happenings, the rain, the Youth Hostel, no parking, the Hotel, no other people staying, just two people, we just enjoyed one another. I started to analyse our evening (why, don't) things are meant to happen.

OK I was eating, fresh baguette, and the end cut of ham. It was always a very reasonable cost, wise and very nice if you happened to shop when they were coming to the end of a full ham.

I wasn't late to bed. I slept after I had beaten two or three shrews that were moving about under my ground sheet, more like I had pitched my tent on their home. Finally they gave up and moved on.

I spent the next two days resting my bum at the beach. I topped up my tan, read my book, and really didn't do much, apart from eating quite a few oysters. Sadly these wonderful days go so quickly.

I was once again moving north, having one overnight stop on the way. I stayed on a farm site near Argentan, this giving me a short run into Cherbourg.

I left quite early making good time I rolled into Cherbourg, a little ahead of time, but it was fine I parked on the dock just outside the Ferry Port.

MY FISHERMAN FRIEND

I was just sat on my bike sunning myself, when a chap appeared over the edge of the dock. He came across and so wanted to chat about my bike and my travels. He insisted that I go onto his boat for a drink. Well OK one small one, I locked my bike. He disappeared over the edge of the dock to his boat. Ooooooh a vertical ladder, I am looking down, and he is beckoning me, so down I go, onto quite a large fishing boat. I got down fine but looking up well that's quite a climb. I followed him into the cabin, well I like a drink but his drinks cabinet was something else. He poured me something like aniseed, wow, it was a tumbler, hold on, he was very obviously a big drinker, and I was not. After an hour, I managed to get away. I had an invitation to visit his home and meet his family at any time. He lived on some island off the coast I can't remember the place. I stood looking up the ladder with the boat moving under me. Ooooh he embraced me, thanking me for visiting him, ooooh Lord the ladder, I was fine going up, it was swinging myself onto the dock I had trouble with. I think I threw myself onto the ground near my bike, so relieved to have made it.

I then drank my bottle of water, took my other bottle out of the panniers and drank that, still not feeling quite in control. I decided to push my bike onto the Ferry dock. I set off my new friend waving until I was out of site ooh.

I booked in and then rode to my place on the dock. It was still early, so I was able to purchase more water. I led out next to my bike and dropped off to sleep.

I was awoken but the Ferry loading man, it was time to go. I thought I had been asleep for five minutes but no it had been for an hour and a half.

Feeling a little better I was directed onto the Ferry. I then tied my bike up and made it onto the deck. Again I drank quite a lot of water and slept most of the crossing. Whatever that drink was, it must have been strong.

When the call came, to join your cars, I was feeling a lot better and was happy to get my leg over my bike and continue my journey home.

I made good time, riding once again on the other side of the road. I called in to see my Mum and Dad then I completed the last few miles to my home. It was cold and dark, I stowed my bike in its garage. My wonderful trip was over. What next?

BACK TO MY ENGLISH LIFE

Back to work, back to dreams, I was thinking (too much thinking). I would like to find the War Cemetery where my ex Mother-In-Law's Father was buried. This was Fillievres in Northern France. I had worked out that it was approximately 100 miles from Calais. I think about a four-day trip. So some three months on, I was once again loading my bike. I think I am getting the hang of this. Once again I booked through the Motorcycle News at a very reasonable cost. I went through the usual passport, driver's license, beans and more beans. All packed and repacked. OK I am ready. I left very early at first light and I was soon around London and tramping on towards Dover. The weather was very dull and I ran through quite a few rain showers. I was coming into Dover and decided to stop at a Café for breakfast, well a full English and two cups of tea.

A CRUSADER

As I was tucking into my breakfast, another biker turned up. On surveying his bike, I decided I wouldn't cross the channel on that, but I knew he was because of the amount of stuff he was carrying. He came in and sat down at my table. He said "it's great to see another biker, are you going to France"? "Well yes, are you"? "Ooh yes I am going to the south of France to see my Girlfriend". "Oh nice, where about is she"? "Well I'm not quite sure, she is moving around with some travelling people". "I am not quite sure, but I will find her". "She has lots of friends in the area so they should know". He then said "I am very pleased with my bike, I only got it yesterday, it's a bit hard to start but once it's going it's great". He bought it yesterday and now he is at Dover) OOOH not looking good. He then went through his pockets saying he had got some money and he produced some small change and bought a cup of tea. I was looking quite bemused with all what was going on. He said, "I am a bit short of cash". "My petrol tank is very small so I have to fill it every 100 miles". "Well how far have you come"? "Well I rode from Swansea this morning", I was thinking what on that? We chatted away. "Do you think you could give me a push to get her started"? I am thinking what. "Yes of course", so breakfast over, we went out to the bikes. My lady was parked on its side stand. His bike was propped against the railings. "What's wrong with your stand"? "Ooh it snapped off when I was getting petrol earlier". I am thinking about this. I said, "What do you do for a living"? "He said I am a Mechanic". "Ooh well that good". "I just didn't have time to sort it because I was booked on this Ferry". "It's not been an easy ride but I will sort it when I get to Calais". "Well that's good". He said "I am having a job to get on her when she fires up as I have all my gear on." "Do you think if I sit on you could push". I am thinking should I have stopped for breakfast? Ooh come on give the lad a push. We started off getting up to quite a pace. I am shouting drop the clutch. He did and we ground to a halt. "Oh sorry, I should have put it into second gear", (well it's got compression) so off we go again. I shout drop the clutch, he did and she fired up. He was away waving as he went, his kaki panniers bulging with gear. I walked back to my bike sweating. OK off to the Ferry where I booked in. The lady said "I just had another bike through here". "Yes I saw him", she gave me my number and off I went, Customs had got my friend. I passed through with a wave. Look out Customs you will be pushing it in a while. I was sat on the Port when my friend roared up, this time with a red brick in his one hand. "The Customs chaps gave me this to prop my bike on". "Well great". His name was Tom and I have to hand it to him he had done well to get to Dover. I am sure he will find his Girlfriend.

At that they waved us forward, yes with me pushing again it fired up straight away. He was going up the ramp and onto the boat. Tom said she starts fine from cold, I do hope so I can't see us getting much grip on steel plate to get it started.

As we departed Dover the sun came out so both Tom and I sat on the top deck chatting and sunning ourselves. I had got about 100 miles to go, he had 800 miles to go. Oh Tom, he is young and tough, I am sure he will be fine. Well I hope so.

We were called to our bikes, Tom straddled his bike gave it one kick and away it went. That was a relief for me. With a wave he was off dodging between the cars. I sat and waited until I was waved forward, and moved out into a warm French day. I was stopped once again by Customs, this time they only looked at my panniers, no dirty washing this time. About half an hour later I was packed again and away. Just outside the Port, oh no Tom was stopped. I pulled up, parked my bike and went over to see if I could help. He had the petrol tank off and it looked like loads of bits spread around him. He said, "Everything was fine". "I am just going to have the carb off, clean it out and also adjust the tappets". "I just need to get her starting a little better". "I am ok". We did a handshake one that went this way and that. I really didn't know what I was doing but we got there in the end. We wished one another all the best and I was away.

FILLIEVRES

I set my sights on Fillievres, the weather wasn't looking too good, very many dark clouds, but it stayed dry. As I neared the village by late afternoon, I spotted a Camping Municipal. I think that will do me for tonight. I then rode around looking for the Cemetery. An hour later and I still couldn't find it, so as time was getting on, I headed back to the campsite, but I couldn't find the campsite either.

A FELLOW TRAVELLER

Twice while looking I passed a chap on a moped with a small trailer. The trailer was homemade, wood with what looked like pram wheels. Finally after riding around for half an hour I found the campsite. How I missed it I have no idea. Just after I arrived the man on the moped arrived. I found a pitch and set to it putting my tent up while at the same time I was watching the action just across from my pitch, my moped rider was putting his tent up, but it incorporated this trailer. You see some smart stuff, he could un-hitch his bike and the trailer was part of the tent. His tent was also quite big. I think he was very French so we didn't converse much but a few gestures and smiles said it all. He was so brown his arms and face, but the next morning in the wash area he took off his shirt and he was whiter than white.

It was now looking definitely like rain. I decided to cook my beans and finish of the sandwiches for my dinner. I had just finished when it started to rain. I fell into my bed with it pounding on my tent. Well it's a good job I hadn't got the Weetabix wonder world tent (I had given it back to the Children). I was soon asleep my day had been long and very interesting.

MONSIEUR

I was awoken by my friends moped, oh is it that late? I peeped outside maybe he has gone fishing or whatever? He was back in no time with two fresh loaves, smelling good. I heard a "Monsieur" from outside my tent. I poked my head out and he handed me a loaf. "Well thank you". He then said, "You're welcome". Well that was good English. I had presumed that he didn't speak English, I now think he just didn't want to. Fortunately the rain had stopped. Everything was very wet but at least it wasn't raining.

So with my sweaty cheese and my new fresh French baguette (it was hot), I tucked into breakfast, and very enjoyable it was with my English cup of tea. I sat and studded my map, well I am sure I can find the Cemetery, it's not far. After packing up and wishing my friend a goodbye, he was busy loading his bike. I was away within half an hour and I was once again looking but still unable to find the village. I finally gave up and went to a shop that sold maps. Well I found a map but it was silly money. At that moment the shop owner came over to me. I showed him the name of the Village and he said it was not far. I knew that, so he drew me a route, but that turning is just up the road, how have I missed that? I thanked him very much as it saved me paying for a map. I set off again, it's here, but after a mile or two, I turned around and went steadily back along the road. There it is the Village sign is covered with foliage. I stopped and pulled the branches away from the sign. Now maybe it will be seen.

ERNEST VINCENT

OK I rode on steadily, I was just entering the village and there was the Cemetery, very small. I parked my lady and walked in. For some reason I walked to my right and there was his grave, he was killed just at the end of the First World War. How very sad! I took a cutting of a shrub on the grave and carefully stowed it in my pannier. I stayed there for an hour looking, and telling him that his daughter was OK, that he had Grandchildren (life goes on) what did they die for?

I rode into the village and parked up, it was so tranquil. There is no way you would envisage a war here, until you saw the bullet marks in the old buildings, the Church had caught it as well. I went to the Café and sat, it was so quiet, and I think I was in a sombre mood. I stayed most of the day. I took a lot of pictures to show my Mother-In-Law.

As evening approached, I fired my lady up and was away. Once again heading for Calais, the weather was closing in, it had been nice all day but now it was not looking good. My tent was still wet from last night, so I decided to find a Bed and Breakfast as it was looking like another wet night.

UN HOTEL BON MARCHE

I found a small Hotel, the price was OK and you could also get a meal at the Bar next door. The chap asked me as normal for my passport then he slipped it behind the desk. I held out my hand (like hand it back). "No in the morning", this had happened to me quite a bit but not on the last couple of trips. I said that I would pay him now and at that out came my passport, happily I stowed it away. I hate not having it with me.

My lady locked up and under a cover at the rear of the Hotel, I carried my gear to my room.

The room was clean and it did have a heater, I will say no more. I unwrapped my tent and spread it out. It should dry reasonably quickly. My plan was if this weather continues as I think it would, I would leave for the Port early.

After a nice cool shower, one of many that I have taken (What's wrong with hot)? The nicest thing in the world to a weary traveller is a good comfortable bed and a nice HOT shower.

I stowed my film of the Village away, I had taken quite a few. I had a snooze for an hour and then went next door to the Bar. The beer was good and I also had a very nice omelette. It wasn't late when I turned in for the night.

FRESH FISH

I was up early and it was still pegging it down. Well it's going to be a wet ride today, but by the time I was ready to move it had stopped raining and I think the sun was looking as if it might shine. I was away and glad to be on my bike. I was soon running into Calais, onto the Port. I parked outside the P&O Office. The girl in there was very obliging. You were on the afternoon one, so she just transferred the ticket. I had an hour to wait, so after Customs, I parked up and wandered around the Port. The sun was now warm so it made everything nice. There were some lads fishing, so I struck up a conversation with them. They were talking schoolboy English and doing very well. They had quite a few fish. They asked, "Would I like a few marcels"? "Yes I love fish", so I gutted six nice fish and the lads were quite impressed at the way I went about gutting the fish. I paid the lads for the fish and they were very cheap. It was pocket money for them. They should keep until I get home (I hope). I was just walking away when a shout went up. One of the lads had hooked into something big, so I shot back and yes he had a very nice large conger. Woo I would like that one. They landed it and it turned out to be a nice silver specimen. I couldn't have stowed it on my bike but this one wasn't for sale. They told me there is one Restaurant Owner who always takes any conger they catch. Thanking them I departed again. I wrapped the fish in a bag and decided not to put them in the pannier as the exhaust runs below the panniers so they would get warm on a long run. If I stowed them at the front of my fairing then the wind should cool them. This was achieved with a couple of bungees. The packing of the fish was being watched by about ten cars, which were thinking what is he doing? I was once again ready to go.

Just after that I was waved forward, up the ramp and tying my lady once again to the bulkhead. I found a nice comfortable seat and slept most of the way.

When I was called to the car deck I checked my fish and all seemed well. I was away, and yes Customs pulled me in. "Yes its fish". "Well take it off". "Well look can't you just feel them", she did and she said, "I can smell its fish". I promptly said, "No you can't, they are too fresh to smell". She replied "on your way".

Out and around Dover I was away on the M25, which was always busy, the M4 was looking good heading for home. I hope my Son is home he loves fish.

LIFE

My house was devoid of furniture after my divorce. It had been some time ago and I had not got around to getting more furniture. We had two beds and a tiny television, which sat in the corner of the lounge. My youngest Son sat on the floor watching it (all the chairs had gone), my bank account was severely reduced but I had my Son and my bike with me. My Son and I had worked very hard and it was time to spend some money, so furniture and new beds it had to be.

MISS FREEDOM TWO

Miss Freedom Two

I then took to doing sensible things (I don't think so). I happened to be passing a BMW dealer (why now)? Ooh I could just pop in. I did and there in all its glory stood this (it was love at first sight) pearl white BMW K100RS. She was just a year old, low mileage, with pearl white panniers and a top box. "You seem interested", said the very uninformative sales man (thinking well would I be crawling all over her, going into raptures and orgasm's if I wasn't) without a thought I asked "how much will you give me for my bike"? What I was going to sell the love of my life just like that. "Oooh you have to be joking, how much"? So I sat for an hour, finally getting a sort of deal that was going all my happy salesman's way.

    The deal done I was analysing my position in life. Divorced, furniture in the house, (we needed it) some money in my bank account, no love life and my old faithful friend, which I was parting with. (But I HAVE FALLEN IN LOVE AGAIN) Love at first sight. I found it very hard to part with my faithful friend but selfishly my love life was just changing, so I signed on the dotted line, just £8,000.00 that I didn't have. At that time that was a fortune to me.

But within a week there was my gleaming K100 RS sat in my garage. It had been love at first sight. My Son and I would take a cup of tea to the Garage and sit admiring her, what could be better? Once more the dreams were returning, (really they never left) with nothing to do on the bike, only change the top box for a carrier, she was ready to go. SHE WAS, MISS FREEDOM TWO.

PAYMENTS

After the first payment I knew something had to be done, no way could I keep these payments up. My Vincent HRD that I had painstakingly rebuilt over many years would have to go. It was advertised and purchased by a German gentleman who turned up one night with a wad of cash and nowhere to sleep. They spent the night on my Lounge floor. The next morning they departed, with invites to visit them in Germany. (This did happen)

TURNING THE CORNER

I was now able to pay a considerable amount off my loan. This enabled me to eat again and to take stock of the situation.

Work seemed the way to go so we threw ourselves into work, this was the right decision. My business was doing well and things were improving. I found a new office lady and happily parted with my ex-wife's office services. I called it my Vincent moment. From that time on the company took off. When my Son had finally decided not to leave and join his Brother in America, he fed into the company so many things that I didn't have. We were away.

My new love was mine, all paid up, Miss Freedom Two was to prove a very trusty steed.

We worked long hours late into the night but this done we would have our weekends, my Son disappearing to spend the weekend with his Girlfriend.

OUT OF THE BLUE

Out of the blue I met a lady. (Yes another but not the metal verity). This became the first test runs for Miss Freedom Two.

So Friday nights, office work done there was a scrabble to see who would get out the door first.

My lady would be waiting, gleaming in her garage. I would fire her up and head across country towards London. I soon found as she warmed up, we felt as one, I was in harmony with my bike.

I would pull in at a phone box and ring my lady to tell her I was 20 miles from her. I would be thundering across country, oooh what a bike!

My new lady would have my bath run, and dinner ready. I had a love like I had never known. She was so nice and from then on we took trips on my bike, spent time on the West coast of Wales, my old haunts with my Children. We had great fun our love life went on for a year. The long runs proved that my bike was something special.

Then one weekend, marriage seemed to be the only topic of conversation. I had been married for over 20 years I could not face marriage again. I ran, she had got me back on my feet and she had made me feel love. I had loved, I was so sorry I had left without saying thank you for being you.

GERMANY

My trip to Germany was now evolving. The plan was to call on my Dutch friends. Then on to see my new friend in the Black Forest area of Germany because of my business I was making it last for just over a week.

My Ferry booked, I was going through the usual things, pack the bike, unpack the bike, my new tent stowed in its new bag strapped across my bike. My Weetabix wonder world tent had long since been abandoned. The new tent was a good length I could once again sleep with my feet inside the tent (technology). It was never easy leaving my Son who by then seemed to enjoy being the Captain while I was away? I sometimes wondered if maybe at some time if my Sons would ride with me on their own bikes one day. After a few years my youngest son did ride with me. Many years later this did happen again both sons.

I was away early heading for Dover. Oh boy this bike is something else! Late morning I arrived at the Port having missed the earlier ferry due to traffic hold ups.

BOXED IN

I managed to get boxed in by four Lorries. It had started as I motored towards Dover. As I moved out to overtake a lorry, he moved out at the same time. Also a second lorry moved up on my left. OK I would have to move out to the third lane. As I tried to do this a third lorry moved in on the right, so I had lorries to the front, left and right. OK drop back, NO a forth lorry had seen my situation and moved in behind me. A bad situation to be in, I was just keeping pace with the front lorry and there was nothing else I could do. This seemed to go on for ages, but was probably only minutes. My only hope was the right or left lorry would have to brake, giving me a small gap to power through. I was thinking it has to be the right one. This happened but there was no powering through, I slipped through, then powered out of my situation. This would not have been planned but they had seen my predicament, the fourth lorry was the one with the very odd sense of humour as he boxed me in. As I slipped away there was one Lorry horn blowing, that was a scary situation, not one I would want to repeat.

Running onto the Port, at least there was no extra cost for being late. I passed Customs with no problems. The car lines were filling up and I had once again been sent to the front of the queue. I parked my bike and nipped off to the toilets and on my return there were four people looking at my bike, so being as enthusiastic as they were I joined in.

"Are you alone"? "Where are you going"? Always the same reply came back to me. "Oooh, I would love to do that". It was nice to talk to people. People make ones adventures, the contacts and the places.

Once again I was waved forward. I soon had my lady strapped to the bulkhead. I made my way to the Cafeteria I had my late breakfast then I put my feet up. In no time I was back to my bike, sat waiting to be waved forward.

MISS FREEDOM IN FULL CRY

I was away. My plan was to take the auto rout heading for Liege. All seemed well, I found the slip road to the auto rout, I turned, ooh no my engine cut out, 5 seconds she started again, um strange. I settled into the auto rout, she was running fine, I only just missed three motorcycle Police. I had spotted a Police car on a bridge, so had slowed, half a mile on they were ready to run down onto the auto rout, no need my speed was legal. Nearing Liege I left the auto rout, at the same time my engine cut out only to restart second's later. I have a problem. I experienced this quite a few times before arriving at my friends, who were waiting at the fuel station as planned. There was Margot and John and we were delighted to see one another again. I relayed my problem to them and John said "there is a BMW dealer close let's take you there".

WONDERFUL SERVICE

I arrived at a very large garage and in no time a mechanic came out. I started her up, turned the handlebars and she cut out, easy. I explained to the mechanic that I was on holiday and would like to be moving on as soon as possible. "Leave it with me we will get it fixed today". Thanking him I jumped into John's car and away.

I was to learn that John and Margot were not a couple any more. Oh um, but they seemed good friends, so who am I to judge. Well when in Holland do as the Dutch do. It seemed that this evening I was going out to dinner with Margot and her family and tomorrow with John, but I was staying at John's house. Having dropped Margot off she said she would pick me up about seven. We headed for Johns house busy chatting about life, love and bikes.

He also observed every female we passed in fact he seemed to know a great deal of females. My new friend has turned out I think to be a Dutch super stud.

HEAD IN THE SAND

Arriving at John's home, it was very nice; to say it was clinical was an understatement, look it's just two nights, just enjoy your friend. He showed me my room, also the shower. I dropped my bag, grabbed my towel and off to the Bathroom. Oh shit look at this. The toothpaste is in line with the toothbrush. What's that an ironed towel? Never but yes, if I have a shower that means water and that means mess. Oh I am not sure about this. As I walked through I noticed there was nothing on the kitchen units, everything was stowed away. I had read about this, but had no experience of it. Well as my ex-wife always said bury your head in the sand as you always do. So I did. My new friend has I think a compulsive lifestyle, incorporating being a super stud. I wonder how that works together. Well it seems fine to me.

I did shower there was a type of mop, so I cleaned the shower base. Hang on should I do this? Well no, so I took a second shower, left the shower base with water in it, put the towel over the bath and left.

We sat chatting, it was good, I didn't ask what happened with Margot that part seemed very obvious to me.

He was planning trips but work was holding him back, not having many holidays he was fitting in runs at weekends, short breaks.

He loved my new bike but was also sad about miss freedom one. With a glass of wine, we both wished her well and hoped that she goes to a good home.

Prompt on seven Margot arrived. They both seemed very relaxed in one another's company, and I found that strange, not something I could do. We are all very different.

My evening with Margot and her family was so very enjoyable. They are a very close family and it was nice to be part of that, although it for just one evening. Margot and I left about 9.30 dropping into a bar that sold Guinness, as I had indicate earlier that I was partial to a pint.

CONFIRMATION SUPER STUD

We sat and chatted. John came into the conversation, well why not half of my reason for being here is because of John. Margot confirmed in her way what I had been thinking (one lady wasn't enough for super stud) so they parted. On other visits I would stay with Margot, we had nice times, many good memories. Her scarf was on my bike for many trips.

My bike came up, well I hope they have it fixed, I relayed my plans to Margot. I had decided to move on if my bike was fixed maybe tomorrow evening or first thing the next day.

We drove back to John's house about 10.30 pm. We sat with tea and chatted. It still seemed odd to me they seem to get on OK. Oh well. I turned in about 11.00pm it had been a long day.

John woke me with a cup of tea and the good news that my bike was fixed. They hadn't managed to get a new part but had repaired it to get me going. When I picked her up they explained that I did need a new part when I got back to the UK. They gave me the part number, this enabled me to ring the garage near my home and quoting them the number I discovered they had it in stock. Great. Strange that this garage, almost in Germany couldn't get it.

I took my bike to Johns and parked her in his garage. We then took off for the day, shopping and sight seeing, sitting at bars on the street, taking in the atmosphere, just sheer pleasure.

I relayed my plans to John, I know he wanted me to stay a little longer, but miss freedom was calling me and I would leave early the next morning. We had dinner again sat on the street. My lady packed, I turned in.

MY GERMAN FRIENDS

I left about 7.00am, John lead me to the auto rout. A long wave and tooting of horns and I was on my way once more. My route planned, I was eating up the miles. I crossed the border into Germany. I headed in the direction of Cologne then Strasbourg. The morning was over cast as I moved further south. It became even darker as I neared Baden Baden. It started to rain, not light it threw it down. I took shelter under a bridge and donned my over suit. I decided to try and find a dry place if only a garage to sit and try my sandwiches that John had prepared for me.

OH NO DID I DO IT RIGHT

I motored on having left the auto rout. Way up, looking to my left I saw many Barnes, well ideal. I turned in and there was quite a wide road between the barns. Slowly moving forward I decided to try to find someone to ask if it was OK to just sit with my bike until the rain eased. I finally arrived at a building at the end of the road that looked habitable. I turned the bike to face the way I had come in, a very normal move when you have no idea where you are.

I looked around and a man appeared and came across to me. I asked him if it was OK to park up for a while until the rain stopped. He promptly turned around and beckoned to another man who had just appeared. I hear the word English.

Well what happened next was unbelievable, the only way I can describe it was like a swarm of bees but not bees, young men appeared around me. Fortunately I had not turned my engine off, they were shouting waving, ooh lord it's an Open Prison. I slipped her into gear and slowly starting moving forward shouting thank you, thank you. They started to peel away from the front of me but were all still each side and behind me touching me, touching my bike. With my clutch fully engaged I was able to do thank you arm gestures, (whatever they are). I was now moving, I can't let them get in front of me again. Finally I was pulling away, enabling me to give them a toot on my horn, they erupted behind me. Finally I was moving faster, only two runners left alongside me. Past the barns I opened up, leaving them behind. I was well clear when I reached the road. I turned onto the road I glanced back and they were all waving. What, did I handle that in the wrong way? I will never know. I accelerated away. Pooh in hindsight what a Pratt, also where were the guards, how can one just ride into places like that? Well I did.

A LITTLE SHAKEY

Baden Baden

Half a mile up the road was a garage. I pulled in and as I did the rain began to ease. I topped up with fuel and sat under the canopy quite relived and a little shaken, happy to try John's sandwiches, not bad for a gigolo.

I think I have had enough of Baden Baden, with the roads drying out I set off across country. This road was quite twisty so the big K was taking it in her stride. Great riding. I rolled into Calw in just over an hour, now south to my friends who are expecting me, but not at any particular time or day, so after a tea stop I pushed on. Evening was closing in as I rolled into the town. OK I have arrived but I couldn't find the house, I am in the right area, but I still couldn't find it. I had the address, so I stopped a lady who was very German, well she would be able to tell me as she lives here. She knew the house, pointing to go straight on and then right, she pointed to my bike saying "Bernard, that's the man". I thanked her and a few minutes later I was being greeted by both of them. It was my first meeting with Monica, who turned out to be a great friend as she still is today.

As I entered the house the sight of my beloved Vincent, resting there in all its glory, greeted me. I wasn't sad, I did it, I rode it, now it had a good home and was cared for. Come on it's only a bike. My Two BMW had taken over and proved to me, far far different, these Beemer's were showing me the world. My Vincent was showing me oil leaks and a very strained right leg.

MY FRIENDS

The Black Forest

Monica took me to my room saying diner was in an hour. I showered and then wrote my diary. As I walked into the lounge quite a few people had arrived. They were all bikers, some of them great travellers. Two of them spoke very good English and the conversation was as intoxicating as the wine. Several of them had been to the Isle of Man TT races, so we were swapping stories. It was a great evening, all apart from one who made me feel so unwelcome. I think it was the drink that had taken over. He was letting me know in no uncertain terms that he couldn't understand why if I visited his country why I didn't speak German. Well he did have a point, the point seemed to be getting stronger with every slurp he took, his look became more evil, Um I could see this was causing quite a lot of embarrassment to all around him. I needed the Toilet so wandered off and to my surprise when I came back he was gone. I was quite relieved. What nice friends. I turned in.

MONIKA

I awoke to the sun once again, and soon after a shower, I was sat with my friends having a wonderful German breakfast. I was told the plan today was to go biking with Monica. Well fine by me, Barnhart was working today.

Well we were soon under way. Pooh what a rider she is, we were eating up miles thought the country side she was familiar with, just great, we crossed into Switzerland, at what point I had no idea. I worked it out as we were looking at Lake Constance but it could be one of three countries I think.

Nearing lunchtime, we pulled into what was a large car park with wonderful views. All there was in the food line was some sort of mobile van, which was selling frankfurters. Well this was lunch. Monica seemed reluctant to eat anything, why I didn't ask but maybe it was too fattening, I have no idea she was very slim anyway. We did sit on some soft grass for some time just taking in the view and resting our backsides.

I do believe I dropped off to sleep for a few minutes. Well I am sure I did as when I awoke Monica was flat out. I think it was the warm sun, the clean air, what a sleeping pill.

We both stuck our heads under a cold tap, before donning our helmets and off again. We soon crossed into Germany, taking a completely different route, fast winding bends. We both loved it. Monica at times was leaving me behind. I think she was very familiar with this route (OR IT COULD BE THAT SHE WAS A BETTER RIDER.) In one town, we had to pull over for a very large lorry transporting a very big earth-moving vehicle with caterpillar tracks. Well I know he saw Monica, but I wasn't so sure he saw me, as the tracks on the tractor came so close to me they brushed my coat. It was quite scary because the driver would have no idea if he hit me he was just so big.

It was early evening when we returned to the house, with about four hundred miles under our belts. To say enjoyable is a total understatement.

Barnhart had our evening meal ready and Monica relayed our wonderful day to him.

During diner I asked them about the French National Motor Museum at Mulhouse. They had not visited it but said it was on their list to do. We worked out my route, riding through the Schwarzwald (the Black Forest).

They were both off to work early in the morning. They thanked me for visiting them, what, thank you for a great time.

They said "just close the door when you leave, oh and help yourself to breakfast". Sadly we said our goodbyes and went off to bed.

NICE FRIENDS

When I awoke it was about eight o'clock. I led there listening but all was quiet. After my shower, I took my bags down to my bike. Breakfast was laid out for me, with a nice note in very mixed German and English, thanking me. So my note back read the same. Breakfast was so nice no just different, the bread is so different. When I arrived Bernhard had taken me to the local bread shop, quite an experience. He said the very attractive lady serving was his ex-girlfriend. She came to dinner that night with her Husband. I do believe he was dreaming.

CHANGING PLANS

My bike loaded, I checked my oil, fuel was fine, and I was underway.

But once again my plans changed, after first stopping off at Titisee. This is the Black Forest area.

- Lake Titisee is located in the southern Black Forest approx. 30km east of Freiburg.
- Size: approx. 2km long and 1km wide.
- The Titisee was formed during the last ice age.
- Just 10,000 years ago, a glacier extended from the Feldberg to the present-day lake. The basins gouged out by the glacier and the terminal moraine now formed the basin of Lake Titisee. The lake is 850m above sea level, 2 km long, just under 1 km wide and approximately 40 m deep. Lake Titisee is perfect for swimming, sailing, windsurfing, pedaloing and for a stroll along the water front.

PRISINOR OF WAR

The weather was so good that once again I toured the area, sometimes my best-laid plans never materialise.

Again I headed across the country. I had many photo stops and a very long lunch break. When I finally moved off again evening was upon me, so I would have to look for a campsite. Well as evening closed in, I had not seen any campsites. I stopped at a small Hotel asking if they knew of a campsite nearby. No nothing, I looked at the price of a room at the Hotel. What price? So on I must go. Just as I was about to pull away a chap came running up to me with a map of the area, pointing to the next campsite, which was 50 km away. He gave me the directions and I thanked him pushed on. 50km was about right. I finally saw the campsite sign. The track was long and very open so any one on the campsite would have been able to see me coming. He did and as I pulled up a man stepped out, walked straight to the rear of my bike, came back to me and said, "English", "Yes". This was the start of a wonderful evening.

He showed me my pitch and in very good English he said, "Put your tent up and come in for a meal".

My first job was a shower then with my tent all set up I went to the little Restaurant. On my arrival I was greeted by the man I had seen earlier. He sat me down with a beer, and started to tell me how fond he was of the English. He introduced himself as Hendrix and said he had been a prisoner of war in England. He said he was treated very well, and always enjoyed visiting England. He had been back to the area of his internment and he had met many of the local people who he had known. Also he had visited a farm he had worked on. He said they were all very kind to him, he was happy to have been a prisoner in England.

He wanted to know what area I was from. Was I a farmer (no afraid not)? The campsite was on his farm, these days he was looking after the campsite while his two Sons were running the farm. He sat with me while I ate my meal, he was great company, he said, "He didn't see many British bikers, so was delighted when he spotted my number plate". He was very interested in to my travels. "What route had I taken"? I told him about the open prison I had inadvertently visited and he found this most amusing, (I'm glad he did). During our evening he would introduce me to various people passing through the restaurant. He and the campsite seemed to me very welcoming, it was nice.

Back at my canvas accommodation, I sat and did my route to Mulhouse. This was achieved by torch light.

I then turned in quite late, sweet dreams, a campsite I was destined to visit. My visit had delighted my new friend. It makes travelling very special.

My friend woke me up saying, "Breakfast for the English man"? I presumed he was talking about me. I crawled out to be greeted by a wonderful day, oh bliss! I wandered off to breakfast. My friend said "Please help yourself there is no bill for breakfast". I thanked him, and off he went saying a quick good bye, strange. The girl in the Restaurant said he had gone to the market with his Sons. She said, "He likes you very much, that why he left in a hurry". Oh well another one who never liked to say goodbye.

I settled my campsite bill and went off to the showers. I was in no hurry as I hadn't far to ride.

MULHOUSE

Finally my bike packed, myself clean and dusted. I was away, realising how long the track was to the main road, quite a few potholes that fortunately I had missed last night.

Determined not to deviate from my route, I was on to the road and moving west. The roads were great, the big four was taking it in her stride and I was soon rolling to Mulhouse. This was my first of many visits and it has changed greatly over the years.

I parked as near to the Museum as possible but was concerned about my luggage. I explained this to the lady in the Reception and she said that's no problem park your bike there. Well this was right outside her office, what service. So bike securely parked I started off. I was just about to read the fascinating story of the museum. I hope I won't, spoil a visit by relaying some of the story. To see so many Bugatti's stored under one roof, there has to be a story.

It seems there were two Brothers, running quite a large business, having many workers, with factory housing, but the pay was so poor. After some years, discontentment grew. Also there was a very large building on the complex and no one was ever allowed near this building. Some activity was noticed during the night hours, large doors were opened and things taken in, always covered up, no one knew or had any idea of what was going on. Finally discontentment and hunger took over and the factory workers stormed the building. The one Brother was killed, the other Brother escaped over the border but not before he had witnessed his treasures being found. They had opened the great door to reveal, a mass of vintage vehicles, the workers set light to one vehicle.

For many years all the money had been used to purchase vehicles from all over the world. In time this became the French National Motor Museum.

I drifted through, trying to take in all I was seeing. I think the fascination was the Bugatti, the one Brother did race one of the cars, to me it was the prettiest one of all.

I was there about four hours, and really unable to digest all I was seeing. Now after many visits I am still unable to take in what I was seeing. Finally after thanking the lady, I went out to my bike, getting ready to leave.

My route was heading in the direction of Basel, not too much time left today as the Museum had taken over most of my day. The road was good so I pushed on hard not much slowing me today.

FUEL

I was crossing boarders, France, Switzerland and Germany. As evening closed in, I fuelled in what I thought was France but it actually turned out to be in Switzerland. I went to pay with French francs, but no chance. It bothered the lady more than me (I had a full tank of fuel). Finally another lady appeared who lived in France and crossed the border every day so she gave me Swiss francs for French francs. That sorted I asked if there was camping near. I got a definite no. Well that sorted I was on my way again, in no time I was running through a very rural area with no campsites. I think I did about 50 miles, this is ridicules no campsites.

HOSPITALITY AT ITS BEST

I was running into a small village, past farm buildings (oh no not another prison). No there was a lady tending to her flower garden. I stopped and asked if there was a campsite in the village. The answer was no, she seemed to be thinking but you could camp in the field. Well great, she then walked me to the water tap and a sort of outside toilet, not used much but fine. I thanked her and told her I was going to get a sandwich in the village and would be back shortly. This I did and was back at my camping spot within half an hour. I parked and was just about to unpack my bike when the lady appeared again. "I have spoken to my Husband" (thank goodness for that). "He said you could sleep in the new barn" (by this time I was convinced it wasn't at prison).

She then led me to the rear of the new barn. The barn was built into the hill so the very small rear door took you on to the straw bales right in the roof, and it looked wonderful. So no tent tonight. The new tap was right there, just wonderful. So after a good wash, I unpacked my sleeping bag and lay it across the bales, that big job set up, I was ready to devour my sandwich. But no it wasn't going to happen at that moment her Husband appeared. His English was OK. "Would you like to have dinner with us"? Did I need asking twice? NO. He said "come to the rear of the house when you're ready", (well landed on your feet again). I tidied away my things and walked to the rear of the house. The evening was warm what a wonderful place to go to dinner. They were both sat out, immediately a glass of wine was put in front of me. John and Domingue were my new friends, dinner consisted of a type of meat, I have no idea what, everything else was from their garden, even down to the wonderful juicy melon, the wine was from a local winery, but I think what polished the evening off was the local spirit. The only way I can describe it is that it tasted like aniseed. "Just have a glass". Yes it was good. I certainly wouldn't want many. Well finally after all had been devoured it was time for my bed. I wished them good night, thanking them for their hospitality, promising to call again. They had told me they both would be out early, so just to go when I was ready or come back the next night (they were so nice to me) I was sorely tempted.

    I did call on them some years later. I didn't sleep in the barn. I was in the farmhouse and treated like a Lord once again.

MOSQUITOS

My morning awaking was so nice, led on my back slowly opening my eyes to beads of sun light finding its way around the tiled roof, for ages I just lay there, I think that night's sleep rates was about one of the best I have ever had. I could stay but once again my schedule was telling me to get up. I had little packing to do, just my sleeping bag. After this was done I had a wash under the tap. I looked in my bike mirror, ups I had a mosquito bite around my cheek. This taught me to always have a mosquito net with me, by midday my face was quite sore and swollen, lesson learnt.

Packed, I was once again on my way in the direction of Dijon and Orleans. My plan was to go way below Paris then up the coast to Calais. My ferry was an afternoon one again booked through the Motorcycle News, so cheap then. I had to have a five-hour run in the morning. Not a problem with miss freedom two. I was well across country by late afternoon. I had gone over my map when stopping for lunch. I should be in easy reach of the Port. It was so hot at lunchtime I did just have a swim in a river, there was no one about so no wet clothes.

MY VERY SPECIAL FRIEND

I was looking out for a campsite, at the same time following a river. This looks nice. Yes once again a nice municipal campsite. The showers were great so this was it for the night. No office to book you in, just find a pitch and settle down. My five pounds a day had slowly progressed to quite a bit more, I must have had it or I could not have spent it. I thought I would eat out this evening, how posh is that! My tent was soon up (no nice barns tonight) ooh well. I showered and was just sat outside my tent, when I saw a quite elderly man walk onto the campsite carrying what looked like a holdall. Just keeping an eye on him, he wandered around not far away. He would prod the grass with his foot, most intriguing.

After about five minutes of this he finally settled on a place, unzipped the bag and put this bivouac up, well this is interesting no sides and no back. He then just rolled his sleeping bag out and that was that. At this time I didn't know what nationality he was. I just smiled as I walked by. I then walked into the town and found a nice Restaurant with a wonderful seafood menu, that's it, mussels to start and the main course was fish. I had no idea what it was but was it nice. With a glass of rosé it all went down very well. My ride was long and very warm today so I made it back to the campsite, ready for my sleep. Half an hour after I had got back, the old gent appeared, he came straight over to me and said "hello lad, nice bike". "Thank you Sir". "I had a look at your bike earlier and I see you are English". "How far have you come today"? "5 hours a long way then". "Well not so long on my bike", he questioned me about everything associated with bikes and my bike, and I was itching to say what are you doing? He was so pleasant and very well travelled. Finally when I was able to get a word in I said, "Tell me a little about you". He said kindly "I have a lifetime". "Well I have been travelling the world on my bike, but these days I am really not up to it". At that, the campsite man arrived, I so wanted to say could I pay your site fee, I couldn't I know he wouldn't have let me.

I am thinking (WHAT) I felt I couldn't ask his age but he had to be in his nineties, "you walk, yes and catch the bus, right, have you always travelled alone"? "Pooh no my Wife always came with me but to be honest she's not up to it these days, so I travel alone". "Right it sounds great". He then said, "Do you think so"? I said, "yes" with the deepest conviction, I did think he was great. We had a cuppa together just talking about our lives. What a crusader, what a man, he did ask me where I was going tomorrow. I told him home. Gosh he said, "That's a long way". "Not on that bike", well I suppose not. I asked him "how far had he come today" and he said "about 40 miles I think". "I just liked the look of this town so got I got off the bus". Oh I was so pleased I had met him, he said, "I am starting back tomorrow, I do miss my Wife." "I have to be up the road by seven", so he needed to turn in. He said good night and settled down. I was so delighted to have met him, what a wonderful man. He had quoted to me, never put off till tomorrow what you could have done today my boy.

The next morning he was just leaving when I dropped my tent, he waved as he left.

What an honour, I will never forget him. I was sad to see him go, but once underway, I was happy. My lady was eating up the miles, freedom. 5 hours and I was rolling into Calais. After being pulled up by Customs I was then onto the Port. Right at the front of the queue again, there was no waiting I was signalled forward and onto the boat. My lady roped to the bulkhead. I made it to the Restaurant I was miles away just trying to process all I had done. The meal was nice, but I was really in deep thought.

After lunch I put my feet up, and had a little sleep. The next thing I knew was they were calling people to return to their vehicles. I was once again on my way leaving Dover behind. The M25 was as always busy, when I joined the M4 I was able to keep to the speed limit so making good time. I arrived home early evening. My lady safe in her Garage, I turned in, well back to work tomorrow.

HOW FAR WILL I GO

We were very busy but during lunch times my dreaming would start all over again. Miss Freedom Two is such a great bike. To ride on the open roads on the continent brought her in to her own. She was built for it so my plans would slowly piece together. Longer journeys

MARGOT

After a few weeks I was in contact with Margot in Holland. We decided that I would go to see her, leaving on a Friday morning and spend the weekend together. I would return on Monday.

ENTHUSIASTIC RIDER

This arranged I left at about five in the morning. I had a good run to Dover it was great to be with my lady once more. The weather was warm but cloudy, so it was a smooth crossing I was soon out of Calais moving quickly towards Germany around Liege, arriving earlier than I had planned. I had made good time. I wasn't in a hurry but the amount of ground I was covering was because of the smoothness of my bike and also the very enthusiastic rider. I parked my lady at Margot's sister home (nice garage). Margot picked me up from there and we spent the weekend sightseeing. We visited Maastricht eating out at great restaurants seeing all her family. It was just nice to be here. Her flat was just a sleeping place I think we only had breakfast once. Maybe this is a lady thing she didn't eat much, most likely on a diet. We were great friends as we still are today.

Monday morning I followed her to the auto rout, we had said our goodbyes, and with horns blowing I was on my way. Once again I made good time and was soon rolling into Calais. I had just a short wait before loading. Off at Dover and away all was going well.

REIGATE

As I neared Reigate, the signs were coming up for road works so I moved into the contra flow slowing for the speed limit at the same time. Suddenly I heard a squeal of brakes and tyres, the next thing I knew I was being knocked off my bike veering to the left as my bike and I went down. I followed my bike along the ground until finally it came to a halt. I was led in the middle of the M25 on my back. The next thing I remember was that another bike stopped. He came over and lifted my visor. I was looking at him. He said, "Are you OK"? I said, "I think so" then I heard another voice say, "is he dead"? I certainly was not. The biker got me to the side of the carriageway then I could see that what had hit me was a big articulated lorry. The biker said "its OK the lorry has jacknifed so no cars can get past". "I slipped through with my bike". A few minutes later the Police and an Ambulance arrived.

POLICE POINT OF VIEW

Because I was alive the Police tried to persuade me not to go to the Hospital, the Ambulance men soon sorted that. I was put in the Ambulance and taken to the nearest Hospital, where a doctor came to see me. He said that they would have to cut my leathers off. "No, no" I said, "let me try and take them off". This I did (it saved them) it wasn't easy I was starting to stiffen up. The doctor then gave me the once over. "Well you going to be very stiff, but I think you are OK" he said. "I have never had a biker in who had so much protection on, not a scratch on you". I was so lucky I found out later that I was flying along the ground between the wheels of the lorry. After about two hours they said I could go. Well now to find my bike. After a few phone calls I got a taxi to where my bike had been taken in the hope that she was rideable.

MORE DAMAGE TO MY BIKE

But no she had come off far worse than I did. The frame was bent and there was a large amount of damage to the one side. My panniers were badly damaged. This saved my leg as my bike went down. It enabled me to break loose. So the next thing I did was to call the RAC. They came and picked up my bike and me and once again we set off home with me feeling very tired and very sore.

The RAC dropped my bike off at the local dealers, and then took me home. Well that was a long day.

AFTER SIX MONTHS

The next day I felt very knocked about but fortunate to be alive. What happened with the lorry driver I have no idea but my insurance kicked in. After the assessor had seen my bike they said it as a right off. Just what does that mean? Well if they repaired two of the panels and repainted them then they wouldn't right her off. This I agreed to. Then time went on, in the mean time I was visiting the Hospital for what they termed as whiplash (a stiff neck) it's improved over the years but not much. Damp weather always makes it worse.

I was six months without my bike. The planning was going on but with no bike to do it with.

Finally I had a call from the dealer, John the mechanic had finished her. I got a lift and once again there she was in all her glory Miss Freedom Two. Ooh it was good to have her back.

MILES AND MILES

My next trip would be to I hope Harwich to Hamburg then Berlin – Poland, the Czech Republic, Slovakia and then on to the Hungarian border. Then return home with whatever route I fancied. Sounds good to me.

My plans were to camp as well as using Hotels, so I would be carrying, the same amount of equipment plus a very large mosquito net. Two months soon passed, the ferry was booked and I was ready to go. I set off from home finding it strange to be going east and not southeast or south. The Ferry was an overnight job, so when I rolled onto the Port they were loading. My lady was soon strapped down and we were off. It was quite a large boat with a nice lounge and dining room. I sat chatting to a couple that were touring in their car. They seemed to have every Hotel and campsite booked. They produced their itinerary and really it was very much together. They said, "strange you haven't booked anything" then, "no, oh how will you manage"? "I am sure something will come along". "Well dear I couldn't do that" and her Husband said, "I am sure he has done it before". "I am sure he will be OK". Ooh that gets me thinking. I think travelling as I do would take them completely out of their comfort zone. I wished them good night and turned in. My night's sleep was good. I packed my one bag as I had left the others on my bike, well I didn't think it would go anywhere. I had breakfast with my newfound friends then went onto the deck. I was amazed at the amount of wind generators there were, it seemed like hundreds. Hamburg looked an interesting place. I think it would be nice to stay in the area for a few days some time.

The city of Hamburg has a well-deserved reputation as Germany's *Gateway to the World*. It is the country's biggest Port and the second busiest in Europe, despite being located astride the River Elbe, some 100 kilometres from the North Sea. It is also Germany's second largest city with a population of over 1.8 million.

HAMBURG

I was called to the car deck. I un-strapped my bike. I sat waiting to be directed forward. Riding off the boat I was in Germany. I came out of the Port and saw a Café. I pulled over and sat on the street with a cup of tea taking in the traffic that came out of the Port, a very busy Port. My lady was parked next to the place I was sitting, this being her first trip after a complete dismantle job. I went around her and everything seemed to be in order. So after going over my route again, I was away and making good time. I spotted the ABS light was coming up so I pulled in. I had just ridden through quite a lot of gravel where they had been repairing the roads and some small bits had lodged on the ABS unit on the front wheel. I gave it a good clean. OK away again, yes all seemed well the light had gone out. Berlin was my first stop and I was making good time. On the outskirts I was looking for Bed and Breakfast and I noticed quite a new sign for Bed and Breakfast so I pulled in there.

EAST BERLIN

The women had heard me pull up so I met her half way up her garden path. I knew no German, she knew no English, but we communicated. She had a most aggressive way about her one I didn't take to. The room looked and was quite nice. She let me know in no uncertain terms my bike was not to come into her garden. I let her know that it had to or I would leave. So with an evil look she agreed, she also let me know I was to be out in the morning by eight. I agreed thinking you have no chance. She wanted the money up front and I told her I would get her cash when I went for my meal. There was no way she was getting the money up front, she hadn't asked for my passport so I wasn't volunteering it. We weren't getting on too well. I then asked her if there was a Restaurant near, I think she said just up the road, she was using very aggressive hand signs, I am glad I took the bike when I went looking for the Restaurant because it was more than walking distance. The Restaurant was nice. I managed a nice beer and a nice salad with some sort of cooked ham. I was in East Germany, not the nicest area to be in. It struck me they were all Russian, it turned out to be about right.

After my meal I found my way back to my very nice, room, I parked my bike apparently in the wrong place as she came out to get me to move it. "Well that's not what you told me 2 hours ago". Still I moved my bike over letting her know I wasn't happy. Again she held up a piece of paper saying 8. This was my time to leave in the morning. She then asked for my passport for which I produced this camping carney, complete with photo and signed, with a wax stamp only common to these camping carneys, (it was one of my Children's printing stamps). I waved it in front of her. She was having none of it, well that's all you're getting. I just hoped she wouldn't notice the little puppy in the centre of the stamp. Finally she wrote down the number. She handed it back. It was the registration of my last bike and my car. (Sucker).

It was very obvious that the room had been recently completed. It was quite nice and after my shower I settled down for the night.

EVIL

The next thing I heard was banging on my door. I just lay there thinking it would go away (it didn't) so I crawled out towel just around me. Opening the door I seemed to receive an onslaught of abuse, so I just looked at her and she slowly ran out of steam. I told her go away in jerking movements and she started on again. I walked back into the room with her following, snapping at my ankles. I turned on the shower dropped my towel, thinking she WILL back off now. I don't think so, what is up with this stupid cow. When I stepped into the shower she left, everything went into slow motion. In other words I took my time. Well after my long shower I stepped out, oh a male person as well, maybe the whole village will come and look. They just stood there watching, I dried off, and I really think this was all so bizarre, including what I was doing. While drying myself off I had forgotten the pint of milk I had put by the side of the bed ready to put on the bike. I kicked it over, pooh I glanced up and she hadn't seen it. The complete pint was draining over the carpet and soaking in under the bed, ooh that's a shame. I just gently shoved the bottle under the bed with my foot, a little surprise for her later. After an hour of tripping backwards and forwards to my bike I was nearly ready, I drained the hot water tank, I whipped the cover of the water cylinder and disconnected the immersion heater and left. That should cost her what I paid for the room. I paid the cow. I think I am ready to move on. By this time her man had disappeared, I said goodbye holding my hand out, surprise surprise she walked away. I really think I couldn't recommend her to anyone. I think she had undergone surgery I am convinced it was a charisma bypass.

I fired my lady up finally at ten o'clock and I was on my way, a most casual morning, most enjoyable. Cow.

The area wasn't the nicest, buildings were being torn down, some of them looked like prisons, and well at least they were pulling them down. To add to it, rain started to lash down, so I was making slow progress. Not having had any breakfast, I pulled into a Diner. Well surprise, surprise it was nice the staff were pleasant, ooh maybe I should go back and clean the carpet (don't think so) it should start to stink in a few days.

I sat watching the rain at the same time tucking into a very nice breakfast. The staff all seemed interested in my bike (but its German) oh well maybe they can't afford one like it. I have no idea but they were nice any way. After an hour the rain seemed to be getting heavier. I needed to get moving so I fired up my very wet lady, and went on my way but the weather was not easing at all so I am thinking of Potsdam. It was not looking to bad, so early afternoon I decided to do a bit of sight seeing. I found what looked like a nice hotel, parked my bike right in the entrance and booked in. The lady spoke very good English, so I asked her what, why, and about the attitude to travellers. "Oh there's nothing like that here we love to have travellers". I then explained what had happened to me on the previous night. Well she had no understanding of this at all but did say something about Russian people. She needed to say no more. I am sure this is confined to East Germany.

My room was very nice, after showering, I rested for an hour, I then decided to take a walk as the sun had come out and the place looked completely different. What a nice place!

Potsdam was the residence of the Prussian kings and German Kaisers until 1918. It is the site of the Parks and the Palaces of Sanssouci, the largest World Heritage Site in Germany. The city is now the capital of the German federal state of Brandenburg and a home to three public Colleges.

The state capital Potsdam assumes an outstanding position in the rich cultural landscape of the State of Brandenburg.

Potsdam, the city of Prussian Palaces and Gardens, offers not only a historical heritage, a source of pride known well beyond the state, but also a richly diverse selection of modern culture and art.

It was great wandering the streets of this very nice city. I wandered around many shops, just really taking in the atmosphere of the very old city. Once again, food shops, I have great time looking at food from other countries. Thinking of food, I thought it is time to eat, they all looked nice if not a tad expensive. I wandered from street to street.

OOOH WRONG STREET
RED LIGHT

Then to my surprise, there in the window was a lady with to say the least (not much cloths on). I smiled as I walked by and she gave me a most inviting smile, (yes I had wandered into the red light district) um well just enjoy the scenery and keep walking. This I did, having many invites to just pop in and see more.

Something I wasn't going to do. Having said that, one or two caught my eye. Try and think about your stomach, that didn't work. So I just kept looking and finally wandered back into normality (IF YOU COULD CALL IT THAT). I found a nice little Restaurant, where they spoke very good English.

My meal consisted of fish, cooked very nicely, in wine, but I have no idea how they make it taste so good. There was a small sort of sausage looking thing for the starter. I had no idea of its origin, or its significance but it was very nice. I did have a bottle of wine, as I was not riding my lady tonight. I had a very pleasant evening, the waitress was very keen to practice her English, she was practicing more as the evening progressed, and it was nice. I left, skirting around the lady's area and back to my hotel. Walking through the city was enough exercise for one day, and it seems there is more to biking than meets the eye. I drifted off to sleep and gone were the thoughts of my Russian lady banging on my door at some unearthly hour, WHAT SHOULD I DREAM OF TONIGHT Dreams to order.com?

I GIVE POLAND A MISS

I awoke to a nice morning. Oh lord it must be late, no about nine. I sat in bed, working out my route for the day. My route was to cross into Poland, then look around again. I packed my panniers, took them to my lady who was happily sat outside the Reception. I then went into breakfast, chatting to the chap who brought my tea. He asked where I was heading, and I relayed my route. He then strongly recommended that I didn't go into Poland, as there were many floods, it was very dangerous. Quite a lot of people had died, he said go farther south and into the Czech Republic. Yes I must think about this.

I loaded my lady once again I was on my way, my head clear and a smile on my face. My lady was talking to me. I headed toward the Polish border. Thinking I must see for myself heading for Cottbus and the border, it's not looking good there were many warnings. I crossed the border. The border Guards said, "It is very bad have you got to go on"? I said "no". "Well don't go farther south". OK more warnings. I turned back crossed back into Germany.

CZECH REPUBLIC

I headed south towards the Czech border and Pilsen in the Czech Republic. I was moving fast, happy to be on the road again. I stopped only for fuel later on in the day. I was buzzing up to the Czech border. Sliding up the side of lorry's bringing me near to the front of the queue. I had no trouble with the border guards, in fact they seemed happy to chat to a biker in sign language. They seem to find my bike very interesting, but its German odd. OK all done just about an hour, they waved my through.

BEER ONE TO MANY

I then stopped at the shops, and Bar, the buildings were just sheds, it looked a real dump, but the beer was good, it had been so hot. I parked up at the border I needed a drink, not very wise having had little to eat all day, just drinking water.

The beer quickly went to my head. I decided to sit for an hour and take a little nap. I think I will find a place to stay it's been a long day.

MY UK NUMBER PLATE

I walked out to my bike she was surrounded with people just looking at it. One lady who said she was Russian asked me to take her picture with my bike. Her English was very good she wanted the UK number plate in the picture, why I don't know. I took several others as they were holding their cameras for me. I am on the German border so they must have seen BMW bikes like mine, so I think the attention must be the British registration. After many photos, I said my goodbyes and was on my way in the direction Pilson. I rode for about half an hour, found a small town and a room straight away with a Café below with safe parking at the rear for my lady. What more could I desire after a great days riding. The man showed me the room, it was very basic but all I needed. The shower worked, that's a bonus.

I sat that evening in the Cafe chatting to a couple of chaps who said they had bikes, but were working in the country and their bikes were at home. They were Germans and they verified what I had been thinking. The country so far had been in a slow progression of decay. It seems that the Russians never knock anything down, but never maintain it, so everywhere you looked the buildings were in need of major repairs. I found this consistent throughout this country. My new friends were builders, rebuilding Churches, during the occupation of Czechoslovakia. There was great conflicted over religion as there is in the world today and most likely always will be.

My meal was nice, meatballs. This seemed to be the speciality of the country, and I must say very enjoyable. Makes a change from fish.

I wasn't late to bed, as my long ride was beginning to tell me that sleep would be next. Before settling down, I sat and planned my route. I was aiming for Pilzen then on to Prague. Yet another bed, well I think it's beating that bedroll and my tent.

After a good sleep I crawled out of bed, first looking out of my window, the weather looked dry.

I was soon down to breakfast, it was a continental, a little sparse but OK. The tea was good so that was a bonus. I then packed my lady, paid up and was soon on my way. Before long I arrived in Pilzen and there was the famous brewery. I stopped and had a look around, keeping my bike in view, as two German chaps had told me the crime rate was very high and to be careful.

HOW CLOSE WAS THAT

Away again, and ooh no a car came straight out of a side street. How he missed me I don't know it was so close. You ride all this way and some Pratt drives at you without even looking, scary. He didn't stop just tore off.

I stopped just to gather myself I was shaking it was that close, I don't want too many like that.

PRAGUE

I then motored in the direction of Prague. As I neared the city I was clocking the campsites, one particular one looked OK, let's hope I can find it later. Well no don't leave it, so I turned around and went to the office and booked in. I told the lady I would be back that evening. It was just off the main road so I should be able to find it. I motored on into the city, well what a beautiful city, Charles Bridge, the Castle, the wonderful buildings. This is like nothing else in this country, either they rebuilt this area first or maybe it was kept in good order.

The Prague Jewish Ghetto also experienced its golden age at this time. The Emperor confirmed the privileges of the Jewish people, and during his reign the Jewish Quarter (today's Josefov district) flourished like never before. The Maisel, Pinkas and High Synagogues were built at that time, as well as the town hall and many other private and public buildings. Prague was home to famous Talmudist Schools, and eminent literary and scientific works originated here. Hebrew printers also had their presses here. The most prominent figure of Jewish Prague at that time was Jehuda Liva ben Bezalel, also known as Rabbi Löw and famous as the creator of the mythical Golem. Although he spent only part of his life in Prague, he is buried in the city's Old Jewish Cemetery.

What a day, I found a nice Bar not far from Charles Bridge, parked right outside, and had a beer. A bit early for a biker but I gave it a go.

I chatted to the Bar owner, well I think he was. He said if I would like to leave my bike outside his Café, he would be happy to keep an eye on her. Also he said a bike like yours, loaded and with a British number plate would cause interest and would bring in customers. Well I was quite happy with that deal. I grabbed my camera and was on my way. I did the Jewish area, the Castle, also a Museum, with trains and cars. That was of great interest to me, the Museum had acquired a 30-40's racing Mercedes. It was one of the works racers, it had been found, stored away in some garage for years, and it was just there flat tyres and all. I had looked out for it to appear rebuilt, so far I had heard and seen nothing of it. I then went to Wenslasse Square, and saw the clock, great. I stopped at many Bars sitting on the street trying to take all this in, tea was coming out my ears.

I decided not to leave for my camping site until late evening, I wanted to have a meal sat on the streets, and this was a good move.

I called back to look at my bike a few times, he was doing a roaring trade. He said please don't move your bike so I sat by my lady for my evening meal, my new friend was more than happy. Charles Bridge, I could see all the little stalls appearing. Well this was great, the artists selling their pictures, the stalls selling numerous goods. What a romantic place this is, it would be so nice to share this with a lady. Many were arm in arm, I am sure they felt the same way. I had a walk. Well I did have my lady she was parked at the Café.

It was dusk as I straddled my bike. The Café owner thanked me and said, "Would you like to come back tomorrow"? I said "maybe in a couple of days", I had other things to do.

I was on my way. I soon found my campsite. I parked up and soon got to work putting up my tent, bedroll and sleeping bag in place. I then took a shower, by this time I was very weary.

Back at my tent I ran through my very busy and most interesting day. Weary, I was soon in the land of nod.

MARIANSKE LAZNE - KARLOVE VARY

I was very late waking, to a warm day. My plan today was to visit the spa towns of the Tsars of Russia. I showered and packed my bike. I ate breakfast at the little Café next to the office. I then paid my campsite fee. I was once more on my way.

Riding through wonderful countryside, I headed for Marianske Lazne and Karlove Vary. This was to be a very thoughtful day the glory of the spa towns, the pictures you conger up in your mind, the extravagance, the greed and the history. I was nearing the town so I decided to look for a quick lunch stop, this turned out to be most interesting.

WONDERFUL FOOD AND TERRIBLE TOILETS

I passed the little Café, just some old wooden tables and chairs outside. I turned around and parked. I sat at one of the tables and a lady appeared, she was dressed in a traditional dress. She did not speak English. Once again we managed with sign language. I ordered what I though was a small lunch. She appeared a few minutes later with the whitest tablecloth I had ever seen, she laid the table, and disappeared again. While I was waiting I decided to look for the toilet. Oh lord I found it by smell, it was awful, my god it's never been cleaned. I didn't bother but took a little walk up the road and had a pee in the hedge. Yes it was that bad. Then the though struck me what would the meal be like? Well I would have to wait and see. Finally the lady appeared, with a beautifully laid tray, the food looked so nice, even the meatballs and it wasn't a snack it was lunch. It was very nice, when I had finished, she gave me the bill, and once again it was so reasonable. I thanked her, paid my bill and was on my way feeling quite stuffed once again.

The countryside was so nice my bike was eating up the miles. Arriving in the town I felt it was not a problem to park my bike on the street. There was no one there who I thought would have the slightest though of robbing my gear, why I though this I have no idea. The buildings were very grand and a visit to one of the spas was most enlightening. It was so grand and reading of who had visited it and taken the waters was quite intriguing. The colour of the buildings, so many colours, the masonry is not stone but some sort of cement, painted, but all in wonderful condition. Viewing both towns is a wonderful experience, so much to take in, one can't, so I was clicking away and saving my memories with my camera.

I spent the day, wandering around both towns. To be lazy and take the waters I think would be a wonderful thing but I must move on. I know tomorrow is not going to be easy but it's a thing I must do.

MY WONDERFUL ACCOMODATION

So as evening closed in, I started to move, the weather had been great so my thoughts were on a campsite. I motored on in the direction of Terezin. Passing through one village I thought I saw a sign for Bed and Breakfast. WELL why not? I pulled into what seemed to be a builders yard, but out came a lady (no English) so sign language and yes she had a room. I parked my lady and followed her, well that's not a room it's a flat, "well how much"? She named the price at the same time writing it down, that can't be right, but yes it was including breakfast. I got the impression that I was the first person to stay there. It was their project hence the builders yard at the rear. It was beautifully done. The accommodation was sorted.

I HAVE A PASSENGER

She was making gestures towards my bike and I thought it was to do with parking, but no. Well what does she want? I followed her to my bike. She picked up my helmet and went to put it on. OK I have it she wants to ride my bike. No she wants me to take her on the back. Yes, well no chance, so there were many gestures, I am saying "no", she is saying, "yes please". I think I gestured you have no helmet. On that she disappeared and returned with a very old motorcycle helmet. I am very particular about motorcycle gear. She appeared to have no gear i.e. motorcycle coat or leathers. I was pointing to the gear I was wearing not thinking that she would have anything like it. Well within an hour she was knocking on my door, with this very antiquated looking gear, but I must say it was OK.

I am now thinking there must be a Husband or a Boyfriend about. I can't quite remember how I got through to her with reference to a man in her life but I seemed to have.

She was off again, to return a few minutes later with a man. He shook my hand and seemed to be very happy with the situation. I then explained that first I had to have something to eat. Once again this wasn't a problem she would cook me something (how is this happening I have no idea) so we sat the three of us tucking into our meatballs once again, but I did not complain it was home cooking. The conversation was limited to sign language. Little did they know I was stuffed from lunchtime, I would have been quite happy with a sandwich! They were quite interesting they had lived together for four years and by converting the barn to a small flat they were on the road to bettering themselves and possibly expanding by converting other barns. Well that's the idea I had from the conversation (sign language). Dinner over she started to put her antiquated leather gear on. Well it seems OK with her partner, I am thinking now how far do I take her? Oh well, just carry on and do what you always do ride. I had no need to worry, straight on was fine, to the left was a dig in the ribs to the left side and right was a dig in the ribs to the right. How very straight forward this was we covered about 25 miles, also stopping outside a house. She hopped off, knocked at the door and ran back to my bike and got on as the chap came to the door. At the same time removing her helmet. At that he seemed not amused, the helmet went back on and I got a dig in the ribs to get a move on. Who he was I have no idea, with her tactile movements we made it to a Café. It crossed my mind again there is more to this biking job than meets the eye. Things come out the blue and how did this happen, but it was just a drink and on our way, we finally arrived back at my little flat. She hopped off and disappeared and I parked my lady. I retired to my little flat, how bazaar was all that, it was almost like she had done this all before, oh well.

Safe in my little flat I took a shower it was great, well it should be it was new. I rolled into this great double bed and again it was most comfortable. This must have cost quite a lot to put this all together. I hope it pays, but the charges they had shown me were very reasonable. Oh well sweet dreams.

BREAKFAST

I had told her not to make breakfast in sign language (but that hadn't worked either) she arrived at the door with a tray. On this tray was quite a selection of cooked meat and very nice looking freshly baked bread plus a pot of tea. Well I was rather pleased that the sign language hadn't worked. She gave me my bill so I settled up.

I sat eating breakfast at the same time planning my route to Terezin. My reason for visiting Terezin was from a book I had been reading. I can't say I was looking forward to it, but it was something I felt I needed to do.

TEREZIN

I don't know why I wanted to go. After packing my bike I was ready to move, I wandered around to say goodbye, but found no one. I then started my engine and sat, still no one appeared. I rode out heading on to Terezin. It is a beautiful drive through the quiet Czech countryside. I felt quite subdued; from what I had read this wasn't going to be nice but this is what I wanted to do so I pushed on, only stopping at a Café for a quick cuppa. I parked up and wandered in, well this was quite a shock, the people in the Café were all quite dark skinned, almost Mongolian in appearance. I caused quite a stir, very white and the odd one out, or was it again my bike causing the interest. I have no idea. After managing to get a cup of tea, well I think it was tea. I sat being observed from all corners of the Café, they all seemed quite pleasant but as I left half the Café followed me to my bike. They all waved as I rode away. Well what was that all about? I must read more about this area.

On arrival I visited the Terezin Ghetto Museum. I had been riding through many little busy towns, however Terezin has lost its soul. Its dead, after parking my bike, I at once noticed the quietness and lack of people in what was a reasonably large town, but yes, who would want to live here, to play here, and to grow up here? At least 15,000 children died here. I walked into the Terezin Ghetto Museum and paid my entrance fee, I was stunned by life size pictures of children from the camp. This is so sad. There are notices around the Museum telling you not to take any photos. I took a few it is just too easy to forget what we are all capable of doing to each other. I didn't get to see the entire Museum, I couldn't take it, and how in the world can people do these things? How could they do this to all these children? Read more on the Terezin Ghetto. Read more on the Terezin Crematorium here. I think I had seen enough. People are still abusing children to this day, what is wrong with these sick-minded people?

It was no problem for me to get on my bike and leave. I just wanted to get away. Later when I was thinking about this, I was glad I had seen this. Why, why, why, do we feel miserable? We don't have anything to be miserable about. The way in which these poor people perished is beyond belief I think I can't and will never understand this terrible evil.

My plan was head for the Slovakia boarder. My visit to Terezin was shorter than I had planned, so I thought I might be able to get quite a way. I looked at my map did my route and was away. By the time I reached Bruno I was looking for a stop for the night, I think my visit to Terezin had taken it out of me. Most likely tired as I left that awful place.

I was passing a lake and saw a camping sign. OK that's it for the night. For once on this trip there was another bike parked up, a German bike. I first found the Bureau, again it was very cheap, but generally the whole place looked cheap. Well it will do for one night. I looked at my mileage 300 miles today, so a good reason to feel a little tired. I pitched my tent a little away from the German couple. They greeted me in a very friendly manner. However, later that evening, I was not impressed by their Nazi songs, neither were most the campsite. After setting up my camp I walked into the town for a meal. The evening was warm I found a Restaurant with seating on the street. I sat outside and enjoyed my smaller more savoury meatballs. I bought a glass of beer, as I wasn't riding my lady this evening. My evening was without conversation. I think I had enough to think about the Nazi songs latter on didn't help.

MY TEE SHIRT

I took a steady stroll back to the campsite and I met a couple that spoke a little English. What started the conversation was my Isle Of Man tee shirt, he was a biker and he had dreams of visiting the Isle Of Man. He fired many questions at me, "had I ridden the circuit, had I met one or another racers". He was so enthusiastic I wish I could have given him my tee shirt but I only had two with me so that was a no.

We parted with a happy wave its great to meet them. As I neared the campsite, the German biker was in full flow with his songs. He was also walking up and down in his long motorcycle boots. The beer seemed to have lot to do with it. After the day I had had it just disgusted me.

I turned in for the night. He finally gave up about midnight, there seemed to be a confrontation with the other campers near him.

QUIETLY AWAY

At first light, I sat planning my route I think another 2-3 hours to the Slovakia border. The drunken German had not surfaced, thank god. I did my standby breakfast beans and a nice cup of tea. OK I must look out for more beans, as that's my last tin. I soon had my bike packed, stuck my route on my tank, pointed my bike in the right direction, fired her up and was immediately away. A few campers waved as I moved away, that's nice. I had been no trouble to them unlike my German friend.

SLOVKIA

The road was good and I was soon moving, my lady talking to me, a great feeling the open road. I crossed the border after three hours riding with no trouble. I had expected trouble with the guards but no problem. Once again I think they were more interested in my bike than me.

RACING A TRAIN

Half an hour and I was away again on a good road moving south. I had turned onto this very straight road with the railway running parallel. There was very little traffic on this road. In fact I had seen no vehicles since I left the campsite. I was just dreaming how nice this was when to my right a train appeared, there were a few people hanging out of the windows. The train was moving slightly faster than I was so I speeded up, this move brought more people to the windows and doors of the train. My bike has very loud twin horns, so as I would pull away I would blow my horn. Well after a mile or two everyone was hanging out of the left side of the train, they were waving so I would drop back, then there was eruptions so I would pass again not fast, just coming up to them at slow pace, this sent my friends into frenzies of waving and shouting. This went on for some time I think the train was leaning my way. There was no one on the other side of the train I was having so much fun. I was once more dropping back and to my disappointment the train went over a bridge and journeyed on to my left, my newfound friends gone. Then the though crossed my mind, it's a good job I hadn't run into the local Police but thinking about it I hadn't seen another vehicle while playing with my friends.

I motored on. Pulling into the next town for fuel and a little shopping. Great I have more beans. I then stopped at a Cafe, but what struck me was I seemed to have gone back thirty years, the buildings were very poor, the dress was very traditional, the conversation with a man at the Cafe was about some motor cycle racer. I knew the name as my Dad had talked about him. The people were very nice, but my bike they though was wonderful, again I wasn't far from Germany. Why, odd, maybe the Russians once again. I decided to push on, as within two days, I would have to head for home. I was running south, heading for Hungary, I rode for another 2 hours, at the same time keeping a look out for campsites. These I didn't see so at the next town I decided to have a look for maybe a Bed and Breakfast or a Hotel.

INSTITUTION OR HOTEL

Well again it looked so rundown but there was something that slightly resembled a Hotel. I pulled in and went up to the Reception, my bike being right in front of the Reception. Yes they had rooms, OK my bike. I need a garage or safe parking. For some reason I was concerned, I think it was just the country in general, the state of some building, the primitive way in which some were living, but everyone I had met had been very nice. I am sure it's OK I was just trying to convince myself it was. The Receptionist directed me to the rear of the hotel unlocked a gate. I rode in, parked my bike. I took off my gear and panniers. A chap helped me to carry my gear into the Hotel after locking the gates. I noticed there was barbed wire along the top of the fence. This place isn't looking too good, the next surprise was my room, well basic or what, the bed was solid, the Bathroom was basic. My impression was that it was bleak. The corridors had concrete floors. If it had been cold I dread to think what it would be like. Well I am here and my bike is safe, I have a bed. Not bad.

    I took a shower. It ran for 5 minutes before it got anything like warm. Well it matches everything else, used, worn out, oh stop moaning and get dressed. Off I went to find diner, well that didn't take long. In the same street there were several Restaurants, I went into the first one I came to, and it looked ok. My no, meatballs, would my stomach take anything other than meatballs? Well I am prepared to give it a good try. I think I had a chicken dish, which was very nice. I also had a couple of beers, no riding as I was having a drink. In between all this the waitress was practicing her English. We had quite a conversation, she was asking me lots about the UK, she seemed to know every English swear word and had no trouble using them in the right places. I did explain that it wasn't the right thing to be doing and using. She then said "I didn't fucking know that". That bit hadn't sunk in then. I wanted to talk to her about Slovakia. Her English was very good, she told me she was off work in an hour. "Could we have a drink and speak more English". I had no problem with that by the time I had finished my meal she was stood next to me with her coat on ready to go (Well I wasn't going far with her). She lead the way, to a Bar next door to my Hotel (place) whatever it was. Well I can deal with that, we chatted away, mainly about her life, she was living with her parents, but her dream was to come and work in the UK. She was asking me how this could be achieved (I had no idea) I really don't think she believed me. She asked me if I was around for a few days, I said I had not made plans as yet. I was thinking she seems very inquisitive. As we left she said she would see me the next day at the Bar. I left it at that. I wasn't too happy about this, so my plans were to move on the next day stayed in place. I took a different route to the Hotel as I was next to it. She was well gone when I went into the Hotel. I said to the Receptionist "I will be leaving in the morning, what time could I get my bike". She said "any time after seven". Back in my room, I packed my gear it was all ready to go. I did my route. I was going to have a long ride. About 2 hours to the border, then Vienna followed by Linz, Munich, Freiburg, Dijon then maybe south to my beach, or maybe the Calais or some other Port.

I was out by 8am. The Receptionist came to open the gate, she indicated for me to latch it when I left. I took time loading my bike, I would be moving fast today, everything needed to be right, 8.30 I was on the move the traffic was light. I tucked in and settled down to my ride. The border came in sight, I have been so lucky on my border crossings, keep your fingers crossed. Too late, well this one doesn't like bikes or riders. You have to be joking, but no, over to the office, helmet off, no your joking, Passport, OK fine. I took the panniers off my bike, what was he looking for I have no idea. He turned the lot out, hope he likes beans, stale bread and my wet washing. I had washed in the shower last night my stuffed bags were across the back of my bike. Why didn't he look at my tent and sleeping gear, I have no idea. I quickly said in my English West Country accent "are you going to repack my panniers"? He just looked at me, handed me my passport back and walked off. I was muttering and grumbling he had not the slightest idea what I was saying. O.K. don't upset the pratt, just get going. At that a second guard appeared, just keep your head down and get on with it. I was back out to my bike, and very soon on my way. I left very slowly as I had no idea if he had said go, I just presumed I could go when he gave me my passport back. The border out of sight I was able to open up and start eating up some miles he had cost me.

VIENNA

It took about an hour so not too bad. I was nearing Vienna feeling a little hungry my travelling life seems to revolve around food, well why not. So I took the road into the city, bad idea, what a wonderful city. I found a Cafe by the river, my bike parked next to my table. The chap that served me was Welsh all the way from Carmarthen. He was studying music, and worked part time in the Bar so we hit it off very well. He was saying, "You should go and see this place and that place". I did explain that I had a long way to go today, but I knew that was looking doubtful, the nice border guard, now Vienna. After my continental breakfast for midday I left my bike with my Welsh friend. I had a few hours sight seeing, it's another wonderful place for street watching. I was topped up with quite a few oranges juices plus many rather grand buildings. I arrived back at the Bar and my bike about four o'clock, my Welsh friend was just about to leave, so that was good timing. He said my bike had caused quite a lot of interest. He said he would be happy if I parked up there tomorrow. I had explained I was moving on. Well my plans went out of the window today, nothing changes. I decided to ride for three hours and find a place to sleep. The traffic again was light, so I covered quite a lot of ground. I was around Linz heading direction Munich. I did another hour then turned off when seeing a camping sign.

MY CARAVAN FRIENDS

Well it was camping, a farm, a shower plus a toilet slightly antiquated, but OK and as I remember very cheap. The farmer seemed very pleased to see me, no wonder the sign is so small I wonder anyone noticed it. I tried to explain to him his sign is too small. I think he may have got it but I couldn't be sure. I set to it and put my tent up, trying to hit the pegs in. It was quite a task as the ground was so hard. I hunted around and found a metal pipe and a large stone. This did the trick, pilot hole first, it was then that the tension went, there was a tare, one of the guys ripped away putting a rip in my tent. UM this is not going well, I did a quick repair on it having some very good tape with me. OK it's up. I was just about ready to cook my meal, when a car and caravan appeared (with English plates). They drove straight up to me having seen my British number plate. "Oh are we glad to see you, we have been looking for this place for last hour" (the small sign thing again). "Would you like a cup of tea", "yes" I said, well it seemed like they wanted to chat, while her husband (John) was setting things up, his wife Liz was busy making the tea and at the same time telling me they had been running late and had not eaten. "Have you had your dinner"? "Well no". "Well in that case you must have some with us" (oh well who am I to say no). The campsite with just me on it had turned in minuets to a Cafe, Restaurant and a Bar (Oh well that's life). I spent a wonderful evening with John and Liz. It transpired that this was their first trip to the continent with their caravan. They delighted me by telling me they hadn't booked any campsite. They were just winging it I immediately said "how wonderful" (really). "Yes, I think that's the way to do it, you are not committed", "Well, I have to be there by that time, that hour, that distance, so yes great". I told them I was supposed to be 4 hour further on but VIENNA, say no more. Oh plus border guards, they both jumped in there, I sat and listened to their tale of woe on borders, Liz was not impressed when they turned out her ladies draw in the caravan. The guards had seen and showed their amusement.

We had dinner a few glass of wine, Liz was a very good cook, plus the Rolling Stones (what more could any camper ask for, (this biking job it's not bad). We were all very late to bed, I even got offered the spare bed, on that I declined. I walked the 5 yards back to my tent. I woke about 8am John and Liz were up. I could smell the breakfast cooking. I crawled out and was walking to the toilet, when a shout went up. "Don't be long breakfast is on". We had a full English breakfast and very nice to. They were a great couple and we said, "We must keep in touch". We really meant it, but we never did, sad really. I did insist on washing up, (big deal), then I packed my lady and was ready to move on. John had up jacks and was ready to move. It was a very happy, sad, goodbye, they were heading to France as was I but I would most likely make better time. I moved on, it is the people that you meet which makes your story. What a total surprise and a pleasure this meeting was. Again this wasn't in the handbook. (Maybe I should talk to BMWs).

I rode hard around Munich, my target today Dijon, I was south around lake Konstanz.

Lake Constance is a lake on the Rhine at the northern foot of the Alps. It consists of three bodies of water the Obersee, the Untersee, and a connecting stretch of the Rhine, called the Seerhein, France.

BREAD, BEANZ AND CHIPS

Keeping my head down, and just stopping for fuel and a sandwich, mid-afternoon, if all went well and my bum stayed numb I would be in the area of Dijon. Late afternoon, I was approaching Dijon, I then followed the camping municipal signs du lac, (the lake) following the river for a while and there it was south of the lake. Um it looked quite busy, but the chap at the office said to go anywhere, so I drifted around the campsite, until I found a nice spot (my spot). I parked my lady and stepped off my bike, walking around, rubbing my bum and hoping to get some circulation back. At that a head came out of a caravan window. "Hello luv would you like a cuppa", so trying to hold my cup of tea without spilling it, which wasn't easy after riding all day. When you stop, the release on your hands seem to leave them shaking and you seem to stare a lot, this is because you are totally focused on the route and road. So I walked around answering questions as to how far I had ridden that day and where I had come from. They were a retired couple and didn't seem to be getting on to well, but a biker in their life seemed to sweeten them both up. After three cups of tea and a lump of cake they seemed to be getting on great. I set about putting up my tent. Chris said "did I want a hand", his wife (Jean) said "leave the boy alone I think he knows how to do it". Chris was nice so I chatted to him as I put my tent up. He noticed the rip but he just said, "I hope the weather keeps fine", me too.

All set up, I took my shower. A really nice shower block, it was communal. I had come across this before so I had no problem with it. All shaved and showered, I started my dinner, bread and beans once again. After last night's meal I am sure beans won't go a miss but it wasn't to be. I had just started my beans when a plate of chips came my way. Chris said "the Wife said you needed it after all you did today". I thanked them very much and tucked into beans, bread and chips. Chris told me they had been away for a month and though they would head back home in a couple of days. I said "hey Chris not with weather like this". "Do you think so", said his wife, (I do) they had a little chatter, really as if I wasn't there, "well we could dear, the weathers not good at home". I butted in, "well look why not just explore this area and go slowly to the coast, if you like an area stay a bit". Jean said, "He is right you know dear". Chris gave me a wink and whispered "thanks mate". They said they had Grandchildren and missed them, "well take advantage of this wonderful weather, if it's a week or two more I am sure they will be twice as pleased to see you". I received another wink from Chris.

After diner we all had a walk by the lake, they were holding hands (so nice). I thought they needed a little English company, I do feel like that myself sometimes, in Slovakia it was OK because I met that girl who (I think was learning English) but to chat with someone of the same nationality as yourself is sometimes helpful. Why I have no idea, it certainly worked in their case.

THE MOSQETOES started to get at me, so I thanked them and retired for the night, sweet dreams, long miles and nice bed.

I awoke and stumbled to the loo, there was a mist this morning, most probably from the lake. I took a shower and had a cuppa, no need for breakfast the chips had filled me up. Chris and Jean didn't appear. The sun had got on my tent and dried it out. I dropped it and packed my bike.

At the moment I was thinking of going out of Lehavre or maybe to Calise, so my route was Orleans, Le Mans, then the Port. I had made up good time, maybe about 200 miles or maybe a little further on than that. My gear on I straddled my bike, fired her up and away. I glanced in my mirror and Chris was stood in his towel waving like mad. I waved back I was onto the road and away. The day was sunny yet again, but there was a bit of a chill in the air. I settled in getting my leathers warm, but I must have a fold in something, pants or leathers, so I pulled in and sorted that out. If you sit on a crease, it becomes agony after a while so best to sort it out first. All this achieved on the side of the road, something I have had to done so many times. OK away again.

I had been riding for about an hour approaching a small town. As I dropped to the speed limit, good job I did there they were, with their little speed camera, I crawled by them and they stared at me. I went through the town, always very interesting, and just past the town sign there were more of them, waving me in. They knew I was coming. I stopped and sat with my engine running. One of them could speak good English. I think that was why they stopped me. They knew a bike with a UK registration number was coming their way. I got the usual, "stop you engine and get off your bike". "Take your helmet off, where had I come from, where was I going"? I gave them all straight answers. Then they asked, "Had I seen a hiker"? "Well yes I see many on my travels". "Had I seen one yesterday"? "Well maybe, you always see travellers". Really I don't remember everyone I see. They were what I would term very blunt and to the point, so my answers were the same. I was warming up so I unzipped my coat. Immediately, one of them clocked my tea shirt, it all changed, he started chatting to the one who spoke English, so he started asking me more questions, "had I been to the Isle Of Man, had I ridden around the course"? They seemed to have forgotten why they had stopped me. The questions had become friendly I was even asked if I had a spare tee shirt he could have. I said "yes I would swap it for one of your police ones". Um that wasn't going to happen. So after a rundown on what it was like at the TT races I was told to be on my way, all very strange. I can't think why they had stopped me.

I zipped up, helmet on and was once again on my way. I was very vigilant, as there could be more of them and not really understanding as to why. Oh well, on my way.

A couple of years later, I was stopped at about 5am on a Sunday morning, as I was heading to the Port to get an early morning Ferry. I was breathalysed and sent on my way. The strange thing about that meeting was there were at least 15 police there, why that many just to stop a few people, on bikes or in cars? Odd.

I motored on, keeping an eye out for my Police friends. I was thinking I will stop in the next town and low and behold there was a market. That's me, so I pulled in at a Café. Once again parking my bike on the pavement outside the Café I sat on the street people watching. The Cafe owner was again happy to keep an eye on my bike while I wandered the market. This market seemed something of everything from junk to food to livestock, so very interesting. I found a small table with what looked like household bits, so I purchased 2 penknives for my collection. Well just ones I had picked up over the years. One bought on each trip. So this became a collection.

The weather was so good, it's just great riding, Orleans came and went. I took the cross-country route to Lemans. Stopping for lunch and fuel, I then motored on passing through some nice villages and towns. I rolled into Le Grand Luce this looks interesting it just felt OK. I was grossly overheating, so I decided to make another stop and take this leather off and try and cool off. I sat in the shade at a Bar thinking enough for today, it is just a bit too warm.

TEE SHIRT AND RED ROSE

I had seen a camping municipal sign a little way back, so I decided to have a look at that, so struggling into my gear once more I rode back. I found the site it was small, just a few small tents. The Bureau was open, the chap said "no problem" but gave me a place number. On looking this was great, you get a small area with a low hedge each side and that's your place. I parked my lady and shed my clothes. Even putting up my tent in this heat was hard work. All sorted I went for a shower and made it a cold one. Feeling a lot better, I wandered back to my tent oh my neighbour had turned up. She greeted me with a very happy "hello", spoken in a beautiful Irish brogue. She was very Irish, very dark and very attractive. While I was brewing my tea she chatted away, telling me she had taken a year out and had been hiking around Europe. Looking at her skin I could see was almost dark brown she had certainly been in the sun. She asked, "Where are you heading"? I said "to one of the ports to cross to the UK". She replied, "Could you give me a lift"? "No, sorry no", "why not"? "I just don't do that, you have a Mum and Dad, Brothers and Sisters maybe (yes) well with motorcycling you need protective gear you're not protected it's not like a car, anyway no one gets on that bike without the right riding gear". "What gear"? I said "look you're not getting a lift from me", persistent or what? "What gear, you would need helmet with visor, a good leather jacket and good strong long riding boots, so sorry no". "If I had that gear would you take me", "NO, look take no for an answer I am old enough to be you Father so no means no"!

"OK are you eating in the town this evening"? I said, "yes", "well could I come with you"? I said, "Yes no problem". "Any way what's your name"? "Helen". "OK Helen let's find some where to eat", so we wandered into the town and we stopped at a Bar for a drink. She said, "It's quite nice I had a drink here earlier". I sat just people watching, Helen said, "would you excuse me, I just need to pop around the corner there is a market", I said "fine, I will finish my drink and come and find you". So off went my little Irish friend, I had a second beer and was feeling a lot cooler and very relaxed. I forgot about the market, I just sat. About half an hour later, Helen appeared with a rather large cardboard box, she dropped it on the table. With a wonderful smile she said, "don't look", so I looked away. "OK you can look now". Oh my God, there she stood in a very antiquated crash helmet, with goggles, (BIGGLES) plus a leather jacket that was in quite nice condition and then waving a leg at me she was wearing a very nice pair of horse riding boots. I am surveying all this in total disbelief. There was a long silence, "well" she said, "well what" I said, "will you give me a lift now", "No". "But you said I needed the right gear". "Yes". "Well this is it". "Have you ever been on the back of a motor bike"? "Oh yes, many times". I was not convinced I am thinking why did I stop here?

"Look Helen, if I was just running you up the road well maybe but a few hundred miles". She said, "What's the difference"? She was right, what is the difference. She knew she had me, "look I will think about it tonight". I saw the look on her face (got him). Leprechaun. My reluctance was also because she was quite young and very attractive. She said, "Shall we eat now"? "I will treat you to dinner", I said, "There is no need to do that". I had gathered that money wasn't a problem for her. We wandered up the road and found a nice Restaurant, just off the main street, candle lit tables. It was nice. During dinner she gave me a full account on how she had acquired her motorcycle gear in such a short time. She had come from the market when she appeared at the campsite this afternoon, she said she had been helping out at a stall (I can believe that), so when she took off while I was having a beer, she knew where to go and who had what. The lot had cost her just a few francs. She said she had bought two pairs of socks, as the boots were a little large. I sat there in total disbelief, also admiration of how she had wheedled her way into my very personal life (me and my bike).

She then announced that she would very much like my tee shirt, "No, its miles too big for you". " I could wear it in bed". "It's the Isle

Of Man between England and Ireland surly you have been there"? "No" was the answer. "I will swap with mine," and "What do you think I am going to do with that". "You could have it to remember me by" she said with a cheeky grin. How could I forget her? She had the tee shirt.

Our meal was very nice, I had a nice lamb dish that I thoroughly enjoyed, and we polished off a bottle of wine. I paid this bill, finally wandering back to the campsite. As we did she slipped her arm through mine, after a bottle of wine and two beers this was quite acceptable. We arrived back at the campsite, she snuggled up to me, we kissed and I said good night.

Back in my canvas accommodation, with only a little hedge between us, I lay a while thinking, should I give Helen a ride to the Port, well why not, just because you haven't done this before, (well not much) why not? The Father theory had gone right out of the window. I checked my passport yet again and drifted off to sleep.

TWO ON A BIKE

I woke about 8.30 again the heat was warming my tent. I crawled out, and stumbled to the toilet. I glanced to my left oh there was no tent. Then I noticed a medium size haversack propped against a post plus one crash helmet, a leather jacket and a pair of riding boots. The ground where Helen's tent had been was very yellow um she must have been here a few days. Oh well, you're thinking too much. My ablutions done, I went back to my tent. I had brewed up and was sat having my morning cup of tea. Out of the blue she appeared. I had decided to give her a ride, and if it went well and we both enjoyed riding together then we could spend an extra day or two riding before getting a Ferry. I was secretly enjoying her company and the effort she had made to accompany me was to be admired. I liked her very much. "Good morning Madam", "Good morning Sir" she said. I shared my tea with her. I said, "We will stop mid-morning for fuel and something to eat". "Oh then you are taking me with you" a great big grin on her face, "well yes". Thinking about it I hadn't said yes or no. She gave me another broad grin and also a shove.

While I was dropping my tent and packing my bike, she disappeared once again. All done route taped to my tank I was ready to move. I started my lady. At that she came out of the toilets like a rocket, running to my bike complete with helmet coat and boots. I stopped the motor. "OK are you ready"? With great enthusiasm she said "yes".

With my bike back on the stand, I looked at her bag. "OK you will have to carry your bag as normal". "It must be tight and not move around". "OK, yes it won't move". "When we are riding just go with me, you must be attached to me, when I lean on the bends you do the same, never lean the other way". "OK, yes" she was fine with that, "Don't attempt to get on or off the bike until I say so" "OK, yes It's a big bike and if I were to lose my balance then it could fall on us, ooh yes I understand".

I straddled my lady. "OK on you get", well we were away, just a few on the campsite were waving and she was very busy waving back. As we went through the town she seemed to be waving at quite a few people. How long had she been staying here? Ohh well. Within a few miles, I knew she had done this before she was tucked in (really I couldn't feel her) that's good. We did about 60 miles I then pulled in for fuel and she offered to pay for the fuel. "No it's fine". We then found a Bar in the town for a drink. I wanted to see how my pillion was doing. The grin on her face said it all. I said "how are you feeling"? Her reply was a very enthusiastic "loving it". She made me smile. We had a French breakfast, with tea and while this was going on I was getting question after question. "How far can you ride in a day, how fast will it go?" "It's not an it, she is a lady". "Oh sorry, what's that figure on there"? "It is a little toy of my grandson", "What's that"? "It's my Son's woggle from his scouting days". "Why is she Miss freedom Two"? Questions, questions, we just laughed. "How do you find your way"? I just said "look at the tank it's all there, also I use my compass, it sometimes keeps me in the right direction in big towns if I miss a sign". We knew we would head for a Port sometime in the next day or two, but we were more than happy to enjoy the riding and having one another as company. This worked both ways. I am sure if there was something she wasn't happy about she would let me know. She had no problem in speaking her mind. I said "There is some stuff at Beyeux I would like to see, so I think we will go that way and decide what Port after that".

Break over we were off again, again and great country, my favourite avenue of trees, so nice to be motoring through.

Just over an hour saw us rolling into Bayeux. The signs for the Museum were plentiful. I was soon parking my bike. I just explained to Helen that I had read quite a lot about the war and was a war baby. I was keen to learn more. She said, "Great", I had thought she would have walked around with me but no she said "how long do you think you will be"? "Will I have time to shop as well? "About three hours",

"OK see you about then". She reached forward and kissed me again and off she went completed with haversack.

I took my time walking through the Museum, for a little while not being able to concentrate, as Helen seemed to be clouding my thoughts in rather a nice way (she is so nice). I had lived with the war as a child. All we heard about the war was that my Father was building planes, so the interest was coming from him. So anything to do with this interested me, but the vehicles and anything on planes got my full attention. I have no idea how long I was but finally I wandered out to my bike and there was Helen sat by my bike. She had been to see the tapestry but the queue was so long she decided to leave it. I think she had been shopping and people watching.

I said "how about lunch"? So away again to a super market, we got sandwiches and a drink. We were riding out of the car park and I was chatting to Helen. I just looked around and right in front of me was a shopping trolley. I did a dramatic swerve and I missed it, how I don't know.

Pew that was close, I stopped chatting to her. We rode for a short while found a river and parked the bike. We tucked into our lunch still chatting away, neither of us said anything about our family or life at home, we just chatted about our travels, likes and dislikes. I was looking at my map, Helen had propped herself against her haversack and was quietly sleeping, not long after her I lay back and slept for an hour.

Refreshed, we chatted again, I said "I think as you are such a good pillion maybe we can go out of Calais". She said "great, OK let's see how we go".

BED AND BREAKFAST

Safe place for my bike

She did say "It would be nice to have Bed and Breakfast, I have been in a tent for weeks". She said, "I would love to spend half an hour in a nice shower with a glass of wine". "OK let's look". About 20k I saw a sign for a farmhouse, it looked a great old place. I stopped my bike and she was off saying "shall I see"? Well her French was very good so I sat while she made enquires. In no time she was back to me, "It's fine, very reasonable, I have booked it for one night". "OK fine". "I have left my bag do you want to leave your luggage". For some reason I said "yes" and I took my gear off my bike. She put the bags inside the door. Once again we took off in the direction of Beyeux. I parked up and we wandered around just enjoying Bayeux and the wonderful weather. Early evening we had dinner, in my favourite place just off the town square. I had one beer and Helen had a half bottle of wine. She said "how do you manage to wear your gear all the time"? She had got very hot riding today. I said, "It's a must, no matter how you feel, you just do it". OK it was time we made tracks, I went to pay the bill but she was having none of it, "halves OK that's the way it is". We headed out on the road we had come in on (I thought) but no it wasn't, I pulled in and we chatted. We were both convinced that this was the road but it didn't seem to be right. All I was concerned about was my bags as my films were there. The decision was made to go back to Bayeux to the Restaurant and start back again, maps were no use as I hadn't made a route for it, time was getting on and I didn't want to be looking for the place in the dark. OK slowly we left the town, I got a dig in the ribs, "I think we went right just back there", she had recognised something, so back we went, yes I think she is right. After a while, I did recognise some things. Finally there it was to my left, on parking up I could see there was another road running parallel with the one we had just come down. Well thank god for that we are here and my bags are safe. I asked, no I didn't Helen asked if there was a safe place to park my lady. The lady looked at us in disbelief it was a quiet country farmhouse why would anyone want secure parking. Anyway my lady was parked in the barn at the rear of the house.

Our bags were in the room I didn't question the one room as we were of a kind it was easy being together. Oh boy what a room! It was just a very nice farmhouse. Not only had a great Bathroom but a Bedroom with a very large bed. Well this is great, we had tea things in the room so we sat and were both so relieved we had found the farmhouse. Helen had also left her passport in her pack, how can I tell someone who has been travelling for months what to do, but I did, always carry your passport in a concealed pocket. Without it you're stuffed. I had a look of OK you said it, now shut up. She then said, "It's a pity you couldn't have a drink". I can't when I am riding and told her about some of my experiences of being stopped by the Police. At that she went into her bag and produced a nice bottle of rose wine.

So the tea went out the window, we sat having a cup or two of wine. The second cup we took to the wonderful walk in shower, that's when I knew she hadn't spent much time on beaches, her legs, arms and face were very brown but that was it, she was white. I called her two-tone, with her long dark hair falling over her shoulders we sat in the shower with our cups of wine, just enjoying the evening. Both knowing that this was to enjoy, the half bottle at the Restaurant and the two cups of wine were telling on her. I dried off and fell into bed. Just after she snuggled up to me. I love my bike. She is Miss Freedom Two.

We slept like logs the sun was beaming in through the window. Oh Lord what's the time? OK it is 9 o'clock and breakfast was up till 10.30.

I made a cup of tea and sat at the window. What a nice place this is. There was movement from the bed. She had spread herself across the bed and was calling out for tea. We sat not saying much just drinking tea and looking out at the world. We were both reluctant to make a move but breakfast was calling. We dressed and went down, we were the only ones staying so just the one table was laid up. Breakfast was French and lots of it. We chatted about what Port to head for, I think Calais, as you can get a Ferry there any time. She jumped at that having not told me her plans when we got to the Port. I didn't ask. I think we both had a very full breakfast, it should last us most of the day.

Back up to the room, I carried the gear to my bike and loaded it ready for the off. Helen appeared in all her gear, she had paid and said "Are we ready to go"?

Just getting on the bike was such a thrill for her, as it always is for me. We pulled to the front of the house and waved to the lady, once again we were on our way.

CALAIS

We tucked in and headed north running towards Le Halve and Rouen then running up the coast towards Calais. I had taken the fast route and we were eating up the miles. I was getting pleasurable digs as we motored on. Within three hours after a fuel stop we were rolling into Calais. We rode into the old part and found a Café. OK this is it, we sat for a while little being said then she said, "Ports are Ports but I know there are some great Restaurants".

TWO DAYS

What about staying just for a couple of days. OK I was going to say great, but how hard will it be to say goodbye. So that's what we did, we found a small hotel with a garage below for my lady. We stayed two nights, that evening we had a wonderful seafood menu, and more wine plus lots of chatter. We seemed to be in a world of our own (a nice world) walking back to our Hotel was so nice, we didn't go back to the Hotel we wandered around, Helen tucked herself into me. This was something I liked and had never experienced. We were so close in such a short time. I couldn't help thinking what's she going back to? I am sure she was thinking the same of me, we found another street market, and yes yet another penknife.

We finally made it back to our Hotel we spent a long time in the shower. I have no idea why, it was right. After camping our bed was so cosy.

We were lazy in the morning, finally out by lunchtime. We found a furniture and household market. This interested both of us there was a great deal of furniture and household things, one more penknife to my collection. She insisted on paying the small amount for the knife. I lost her at times, but she would appear at my side after a while. She would say, "I am back darling". (I am sure this was her very acute sense of humour) it was nice.

We were out quite late the last evening. After we had done our packing. We went back to the same Restaurant and the same menu and wine. We had a great evening. As we walked back I said, "I am leaving very early". She gave a big sigh, she seemed OK with that but I knew she was struggling. We once again retired to the shower finishing off the bottle of wine we fell into bed.

My early start didn't work out I woke about nine. I looked around and called, no answer. Looking around her leather coat was hung over the chair, helmet and goggles and her boots were standing by the chair. I walked over to the window. There were my bike keys and one red rose. My Manx tee shirt I said she could have had gone, I never saw her again.

I was running down to the Port, unconsciously looking for a hiker with long dark hair. I didn't see her. I went to the P&O Office and was booked onto the next Ferry. It was loading, I fired up my lady and after Customs waved me through, I was directed straight onto the Ferry. I relaxed on the deck of the Ferry, as again it was a nice day. A couple came over and said "We saw you ride onto the ferry". They wanted to know where I had been, I chatted but for once my heart wasn't in it. Nothing lasts forever.

HOME

The call came to join your vehicles and I was sat waiting to go, letting the cars close to me leave first. I was then waved forward I was around the Port and going through Customs. Once again they pulled me in. I really didn't feel like having to unpack yet again but they just made me open one pannier. As I did this I noticed an envelope, I stopped and opened it. It was from Helen, a photo and a letter not a note. I stood and read it oblivious of the Customs Officers around me. Then one gave me a nudge and said, "OK you can go". I treasured that letter and photo for many years, but when moving house, it went missing. I still have my memories.

I was out of the Port and away, tramping towards London my lady talking to me. Onto the M4 now heading west to my home.

MY STORY CONTINUES

Col de Pailhères

I was on the final pages of this book working alone at my little home in Southern France. I had been writing for over a week. One morning I though that's enough I need to get away for a day. I left my home about 10am riding in the direction of Andorra. After about two hours I stopped at Ax-Les-Thermes at a Café. I was just sat enjoying the day. I didn't see another bike arrive but as I left the Café I saw it parked. It was a very nice red BMW 600. I was stood chewing on my sandwich as a young lady walked up to me and said "Hello". She was the rider of the red machine. We chatted she was Catalan, living in Andorra city. She questioned me as to where I was from and also about my travels. She told me she had been riding for three years and this was her first bike. She was out for a day's riding. I was about to leave saying "I was going over the Col-de-Pailhères". She said, "That's the way I am going". We decided to ride together. The long twisting winding road to the summit is quite something, you have to keep your wits about you as some of the bends are so tight you have no speed, you are almost footing your bike around. It was a pleasure to follow her. Finally at the summit we stopped chatted and took some photos. I shared my sandwiches with her. We then decided to spend the day together riding the Cols and the valleys. It's autumn and the colours are incredible changing with the light every minute. We would stop and chat not really able to take in what we were seeing. Finally late afternoon we ended up at a Café at a ski village enthusing on what a wonderful time we both had. What great biking! We left, she went east and I motored west. A meeting like this only comes about because there were two bikes a red one and a red one.

Thank you Eva for a great day.

Mark

Life is to live
Life is to Travel
Life is to share
Life is an adventure.
Life is to care.
Life is love, Faith, Fairness, and Truth

My Dear friend said as he walked from the campsite, carrying his holdall. Never put off until tomorrow what you can do today. He waved.

Mark Cheney

Thank you Lynn - My children - Tig - Annina for your support and help with my book. My Special thanks to Rockposh.

www.markcheney.co.uk

kramcheney@gmail.com

www.ingramcontent.com/pod-product-compliance
Lightning Source LLC
Chambersburg PA
CBHW060524100426
42743CB00009B/1426